"One of the most imaginative che.. .. ..g..
Christian Millau

After three years' apprenticeship with the Troisgros
brothers, Guy Savoy worked in Paris, Geneva and New
York before opening his first Paris restaurant in 1980 and
his second in 1987, *Guy Savoy* in rue Troyon. In the space
of three years he has won 3 toques and 18/20 in the Gault-
Millau guide. In 1985 he was awarded two Michelin stars.

Guy Langlois is a highly respected writer and food critic and
has many articles on food and cookery published.

VEGETABLE MAGIC

Guy Savoy with Guy Langlois

HEADLINE

First published in Great Britain in 1987 by Ebury Press
Division of the National Magazine Company Limited

First published in paperback in Great Britain in 1988 by
HEADLINE BOOK PUBLISHING PLC

First published in 1986 by Libraire Plon, Paris

Text © 1986 Libraire Plon
Translation and design © 1987
The National Magazine Company Limited

ISBN 0-7472-3161-3

Translated by Rosemary Minett-Sandham
This edition edited by Veronica Sperling and Helen Dore
Design by Bridgewater Associates
Illustrations by Vana Haggerty

Printed and bound in Finland
by Werner Söderström Oy

HEADLINE BOOK PUBLISHING PLC
Headline House
79 Great Titchfield Street
London W1P 7FN

·CONTENTS·

◆INTRODUCTION◆

VEGETABLES ARE AMONG the most attractive ingredients available to the cook – for a host of reasons. They are not fattening, they are easy to digest, and satisfy our natural craving for fresh greens. While it is true that a delicious plateful of young green beans and a bowl of crisp lettuce cannot really replace the benefits of a country walk, healthwise, they do create an aura of well-being and freshness. In fact, we think of vegetables as synonymous with good health. But what are the actual benefits vegetables bring?

Vegetables provide fibre, Vitamins A, B and C and minerals such as potassium, calcium, iron, copper and zinc.

In health terms, we can make a more definite statement; over a period of thirteen years, Professor Hirayama studied some 250,000 Japanese. He concluded that those who did not regularly eat vegetables were 50 per cent more likely to develop a fatal cancer (particularly stomach cancer) than those who enjoyed a balanced diet. The Japanese government was sufficiently impressed by this study to launch a major publicity campaign and take steps to increase the use of green vegetables in institutional restaurants. The code for the campaign was 'Project Popeye'. Long live spinach!

Another advantage of vegetables is their price, which is very reasonable in relation to that of other foods. A well-prepared country-style soup can provide a one-pot meal for 8, for less than the cost of a steak meal for 2! In the same way, asparagus in season is no more costly than many convenience foods or charcuterie.

Moreover, vegetables are easy to prepare. Once one has accepted that they are generally best served *al dente* – still slightly crisp – and that they should not be left to cook unattended, few vegetable recipes require any specialized skill.

Our taste for vegetables has also been stimulated by the appearance of new and exciting varieties in our shops and markets. At one time we ate fruit and vegetables only when they were in season. Oranges, clementines and bananas were Christmas luxuries – Jules Renard, born in 1864, recorded that he was 30 years old when he first tasted a banana!

The post-war arrival of immigrants from Asian and African countries, and from Italy and Portugal, was followed by the importation of new and different vegetables; chick peas, Spanish beans, soya beans, yams, sweet potatoes, broccoli, fennel and mange-tout (snow peas) are but a few. Many of us have discovered new vegetables in Indian, Chinese and other ethnic restaurants, which we then wish to eat at home. Market gardeners and importers have not been slow in responding to this stimulus.

The variety of salad vegetables available commercially has increased considerably; cos (romaine), and iceberg lettuces, plain and curly endive, mesclun, batavia and oak-leaf lettuce all bring variety to our salads.

Another vegetable which has had considerable impact is the avocado, particularly as exported by the Israelis. Mme Mathilde, a supervisor at Rungis fruit and vegetable market for one of the major wholesalers, recalls that 'The first time I saw one, I wondered how anyone could eat such an object. It was hard and tasteless. So I put the box aside. But before I got round to throwing the contents out, I tasted another pear. It was nothing like the first one – it was absolutely delicious. The grower had thought of everything . . . . except to explain that avocados should not be eaten until they are fully ripe!' Nor are the Israelis wedded to the production of avocados only; they have widened their range of produce, and were amongst the first growers to use air freight to bring us out of season vegetables.

Today's greatest all-round traveller in the vegetable kingdom is undoubtedly the French (green) bean. Winter supplies come from Kenya and parts of French-speaking Africa, and the time lapse between their being picked and arriving in the markets of a large town can be as short as 24–48 hours. The first European beans on the market are those from Italy in March; as the spring and summer advance, other areas come into production, until late September, by which point European supplies dwindle once more and again rely on African imports.

The tomato is a rather sad case. Supplies are available throughout the year, yet those which come to us out of season and without the benefit of ripening sun can be dismally tasteless. Few restaurateurs are misled into serving them out of season. Why, then, are they so widely available in the shops? 'Well, they are red, like summer vegetables, and they make you think of freshness,' replied a housewife caught in the act of buying these sorry specimens.

◇ HERBS ◇

Fresh vegetables need fresh seasoning. Heightened interest in vegetable cookery has increased demand for fresh herbs, combining flavour and health.

Basil is the safest of tranquillizers. As early as the second century, it was recommended by Pliny the Younger as a remedy for epilepsy, and thanks to its essential oils, it combats anxiety and helps insomnia resulting from overtiredness.

Parsley combats fatigue and promotes healthy growth in children. Lucie Randouin, an eminent specialist in alimentary hygiene, believes that it is 'one of the most precious health-giving foods that nature has put at man's disposal'. It is worth remembering that 5 g ($\frac{1}{5}$ oz) parsley is extremely rich in Vitamins A, C, potassium, calcium, magnesium and iron.

Tarragon will cure hiccups, as was proved by Louis of Bavaria. His doctors were unable to cure him of an acute attack of hiccups, so he sought the help of an ostler credited with supernatural powers. This unorthodox adviser administered a tisane based on tarragon which promptly cured the royal hiccups, and ever since then doctors have recognized the value of his method.

Sage is a powerful stimulant to the digestion. It is widely used to flavour some of the richer dishes from the Midi.

◇ A CHEF'S ADVICE ◇

Human nature is such that the things you do well are those you enjoy doing. If cooking is only a burden to you, don't entertain at home; if you want your friends to enjoy themselves, organize a visit to a restaurant, rather than inflict on them a complicated and catastrophic meal at home!

Make full use of your recipes. Read them carefully before starting work. Try to work out why certain ingredients have been combined, what effect they have on each other, why a particular cooking method was chosen. The recipe should sound appetizing before you even embark on it!

Try to recognize the points common to different recipes, and to make connections between them.

Use only first-rate ingredients – with good-quality potatoes and cream, you'll make a sublime gratin dauphinois; with second-rate vegetables, however many of them you may have, the end result as well can only be second rate.

For each of the vegetables featured in this book, advice is given on how to recognize the best of the crop. Read this advice closely and stick to it. Above all, beware of vegetables which are not in season; fresh (green) beans air-freighted in from Africa may be excellent, but the only thing which winter tomatoes have to recommend them is their colour!

Whether you are cooking roast meat or chicken, fish, or oven-braised vegetables, make sure that the dish you use is of a suitable size for the contents. It is important for food to simmer slowly, so that the natural juices reduce and become progressively concentrated.

When a recipe tells you to 'taste for seasoning' it means that you should dip your finger in the sauce, taste and add salt and/or pepper as required. This gesture is common to cooks everywhere and also allows you to gauge the temperature and consistency of the sauce more accurately than any other method.

It is a mistake to think that stocks, whether liquid or jellied, are the prerogative of the professional cook. It is true that they require long, slow cooking, but a few spoonfuls of the appropriate stock – veal, chicken, fish or vegetable – can totally transform a recipe.

Remind yourself that time spent on preparing stocks will be well spent, for no commercial stock cube can ever be as full of flavour as stock you have made yourself, using vegetables, seasonings and bones which have simmered for hours in a large saucepan.

A sauce or a cream is reduced in order to concentrate it. But too often one can hesitate and not take the process far enough, for fear of seeing the sauce burn or curdle, especially when the preparation is cream-based. However, you run no risks if you allow double (heavy) cream to boil. It will liquefy, then thicken into a smooth sauce, which is exactly what is required.

Where you are told to reduce or boil off a liquid until the contents of the pan are almost dry, be brave and do just that. You obviously must not allow the contents of the pan to burn, but you must give them a chance to dry out.

A hot dish should be really hot when served and when eaten. However, you have only one pair of hands, and a limited space to cook in. So it must become a reflex action to turn on the oven at its lowest setting, and to have ready on the hob (stove top) a large pan of hot water which you can use as a bain-marie (water bath) to keep things warm.

Use kitchen (aluminium) foil to cover food and keep it warm, without drying out.

One last vital point: hot food will not be enjoyable if your serving dishes, and the guests' plates, have not been pre-heated too.

◇ EQUIPMENT ◇

Good cooking needs the right sort of equipment. If you can find a shop selling catering equipment to professionals, use it; your money will be well spent. A heavy copper-based stainless steel saucepan will cost you three times as much as an ordinary household pan, but it will also last a lifetime.

This list contains the basic equipment that I would really advise you to build up. It will allow you to tackle all the recipes in this book, and a great many others too.

◇ 5 SAUCEPANS, from a very small one for sauces, right up to the largest size you can find. The largest three, at least, should have lids.

◇ 3 FRYING PANS, large, medium and small, preferably stainless steel with copper base, as this diffuses heat best.

◇ 2 SAUTE PANS, with lid. Non-stick finishes are available.

◇ 2 CASSEROLES, one round and one oval, preferably cast-iron. Some models have a lid which can be filled with water, allowing you to leave the contents simmering for hours without fear of the contents drying out.

◇ 2 GRATIN DISHES, oval. Choose flameproof dishes.

◇ 2 ROASTING PANS, for cooking chickens, roast meat, etc. One should be as large as possible, so that it can double as a bain-marie (water bath).

◇ 1 STEAMER/COUSCOUSSIER. The lower half can also be used as a stockpot.

◇ 1 FINE CONICAL SIEVE (CHINOIS).

◇ 1 COLANDER/LARGE SIEVE OR STRAINER.

◇ 2 LADLES, 1 large, 1 small and 1 SKIMMING LADLE.

◇ 4 BOWLS, 2 large and 2 small, pyrex or stainless steel.

◇ 1 FLAN TIN (QUICHE PAN).

◇ 2 TERRINES, glazed earthenware.

◇ 8 SMALL RAMEKINS.

◇ 1 HAND WHISK (BALLOON OR ROTARY).

◇ 1 ELECTRIC FOOD PROCESSOR with accessories.

◇ 1 MOULINETTE (food mill).

◇ 1 MANDOLINE CUTTER for slicing vegetables finely.

◇ 1 CHOPPING BOARD.

◇ 2 FLEXIBLE RUBBER SPATULAS, for scraping mixture from bowls.

◇ 1 GRATER.

◇ 2 WOODEN SPOONS.

◇ 2 WOODEN SPATULAS.

◇ KNIVES:
1 SHARP CHEF'S KNIFE for cutting up meat, chicken, etc.
1 LARGE VEGETABLE OR SLICING KNIFE, with a slightly arched blade which facilitates use on a chopping board.
SEVERAL SMALL GENERAL PURPOSE KNIVES FOR PEELING, paring, etc.

1 FLUTING/CHANNELLING KNIFE for cutting decorative strips from fruit and vegetables.

◇ 1 POTATO PEELER (or 2, to provide for a helper).

◇ 1 CUTLET BAT (MALLET) or heavy knife for flattening pieces of meat.

◇ 1 PAIR TONGS for turning and lifting meat without burning yourself or piercing the meat.

◇ INTRODUCTION TO THE RECIPES ◇

This collection of recipes is not based on Guy Savoy's restaurant cooking; rather, it is a practical book of simple, delicious food, accessible to the amateur cook.

The recipes illustrate to perfection Guy Savoy's spontaneous approach to food. By using vegetables in many different ways, as side dishes, flavourings and main dishes too, he juggles tastes and textures; subtly mingling flavours and creating exciting contrasts of smoothness and crunchiness, sweet and sharp, hot and cold.

Guy Savoy has one great ambition: to help you get the very best from the vegetables you prepare, every time you cook. Many of the recipes are original, but you will also find here his professional interpretation of such simple dishes as puréed celeriac and a salad of French (green) beans. *Vegetable Magic* is not a bedside cookery book, it is the sort of book that should live in the kitchen, where you can flick through it each time you head for the greengrocer's shop.

THE PUBLISHER

VEGETABLE
·FRUITS·

✦ AUBERGINES ✦

EGGPLANTS

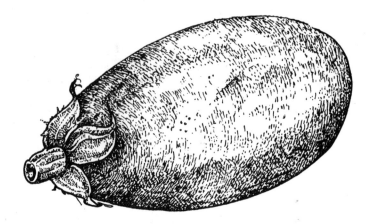

L IKE THE TOMATO, the aubergine (eggplant) is a member of the family
Solanaceae, some of which are poisonous. Thus its first appearance in
Europe, in the thirteenth century, was greeted with suspicion.

In Africa the aubergine had been grown before the Middle Ages. In Europe,
it came first to Spain, brought, like so many other innovations, by the Arabs. It
spread throughout Mediterranean Europe, as a decorative plant. It was not
until the early nineteenth century that the aubergine entered the European diet.

Aubergines are low in calories; they contain mostly water with very little
protein but a little carbohydrate and fibre. There is no oil in them at all. When
boiled, the aubergine is highly digestible; combined with oils or fats, it reacts
like blotting paper, and can become unpleasantly heavy and indigestible.

The aubergine is a tall plant with superb purplish-blue flowers; it flourishes
in a hot climate, but cannot withstand drought. The names of some of the
varieties grown in Europe sound like a roll-call of nightclub showgirls:
'Violette de Barbentane', 'Monstrueuse de New York', 'Ronde de Chine' and
'Belle de Toulouse'. Almost all the aubergines grown and sold in Western
Europe are a deep purplish-black. Further afield one may come across pale
lavender, white or striped varieties.

◇ BUYING AUBERGINES ◇

Look for firm, smooth specimens with a shiny, unblemished skin. Choose
small aubergines, if possible. Beware the small prickles around the stalks of
some varieties; the sharper they are, the fresher the aubergine. Allow 225 g
(8 oz) aubergine per person.

◇ SERVING AUBERGINES ◇

Serve with other vegetables, most notably tomatoes and courgettes (zucchini).

◇ PREPARING AUBERGINES ◇

Slice the aubergine, peeled or unpeeled, as specified in the recipe. Sprinkle the slices with salt and put them into a colander. Set this tilted over a plate in the sink. This will extract some of the water content and remove any bitterness. Rinse and dry the slices before using.

Aubergines may also be cooked in the skin, by boiling, or by roasting over a gas flame. Prick the skin, as you would a sausage, to prevent the aubergine from exploding as the water inside turns to steam.

◇ AUBERGINE (EGGPLANT) CAVIAR ◇

Aubergine caviar may be served as an accompaniment to cold dishes, as part of a selection of salads, or on toast or biscuits as a cocktail snack.

◇ Heat the oven to 200°C (400°F/Gas Mark 6).

◇ Cut the aubergines in half lengthways. Brush them well with olive oil. Place on a baking tray and cook in the oven for 20–25 minutes, until tender.

◇ Allow the aubergines to cool slightly, then scoop out the flesh with a spoon. Chop it into small dice. When cool, chill in the refrigerator.

◇ Skin and seed the tomatoes. Chop the flesh into small dice. Peel and finely chop the shallot and spring onion. Add to the diced tomato.

◇ Mix the chopped tomato mixture with the aubergine. Add the olive oil and the herbs. Return to the refrigerator and chill very thoroughly.

◇ Whip the cream until slightly thickened; it should not be too stiff. Just before serving, fold the cream into the aubergine and tomato mixture. Season the aubergine caviar to taste with salt and pepper.

INGREDIENTS

450 g (1 lb) aubergines (eggplants)
450 g (1 lb) tomatoes
1 shallot
1 spring onion (scallion)
20 ml (4 tsp) olive oil
30 ml (2 tbsp) chopped parsley or chervil
150 ml (5 fl oz/⅔ cup) double (heavy) cream
salt and pepper

SIDE DISH OR COCKTAIL SNACK

SERVES 4–8
Preparation: 15–20 minutes
Cooking: 20 minutes
Difficulty: ★★
Cost: ★

UTENSILS

1 baking tray
1 bowl
1 balloon whisk
OVEN
200°C (400°F/Gas Mark 6)

◇ AUBERGINES (EGGPLANTS) WITH A MUSHROOM STUFFING ◇

◇ Heat the oven to 200°C (400°F/Gas Mark 6).

◇ Prick the aubergines all over. Put them on a baking tray and cook in the oven for 15–20 minutes, until tender. Cut the aubergines in half lengthways, taking care not to damage the skins.

◇ While the aubergines are cooking, wash and finely slice the mushrooms. Peel and finely chop the shallot. Sweat the shallot gently in the butter in a sauté pan until transparent. Add the mushrooms and season with salt and pepper. Cook until the mushrooms have exuded their juices.

◇ Remove the pan from the heat. Spoon the pulp from the aubergines into it. Add the eggs and mix all together well. Check the seasoning.

◇ Put the aubergine skins into a greased ovenproof dish. Fill them with the aubergine and mushroom mixture and sprinkle with breadcrumbs. Brown in the oven for 10 minutes.

INGREDIENTS

4 small aubergines (eggplants)
250 g (9 oz) mushrooms
1 shallot
50 g (2 oz/4 tbsp) butter
2 eggs
dried breadcrumbs

FIRST COURSE

SERVES 4
Preparation: 5 minutes
Cooking: 30 minutes
Difficulty: *
Cost: *

UTENSILS

1 sauté pan
1 small sharp knife
1 baking tray
1 ovenproof dish
OVEN
200°C (400°F/Gas Mark 6)

◇ AUBERGINES (EGGPLANTS) WITH GARLIC AND BASIL ◇

If the sauce which accompanies the aubergines can be prepared a few hours in advance, the flavour will develop more fully.

◇ Peel the garlic cloves. Cut them in half lengthways and remove the small green shoot from the centre. Chop the garlic and basil finely. Add salt and pepper. Put the mixture into a mortar or small bowl. Add the oil and mix well to form a purée.

◇ Heat the oven to 200°C (400°F/Gas Mark 6).

◇ Prick the aubergines all over and put them on a baking tray. Cook in the oven for 20–30 minutes, until tender. Cut them in half lengthways. Coat the aubergine halves with the basil and garlic sauce and serve hot. These are best eaten with a spoon.

INGREDIENTS

2 garlic cloves
1 bunch of basil
75 ml (3 fl oz/5 tbsp) olive oil
4 small aubergines (eggplants)

FIRST COURSE

SERVES 4
Preparation: 25 minutes
Cooking: 20 minutes
Difficulty: *
Cost: *

UTENSILS

1 baking tray
1 pestle and mortar
OVEN
200°C (400°F/Gas Mark 6)

◇ AUBERGINES (EGGPLANTS) WITH A MEAT STUFFING ◇

◇ Heat the oven to 200°C (400°F/Gas Mark 6).

◇ Prick the aubergines all over. Put them on a baking tray and cook in the oven for 15–20 minutes, until tender. Cut the aubergines in half lengthways, taking care not to damage the skins.

◇ Peel and finely chop the shallot. Sweat it gently in the butter in a large sauté pan until transparent. Add the sausagemeat and fry for 10 minutes, breaking up the lumps of meat to ensure that all of it cooks evenly. Add the minced beef or lamb and cook for a further 10 minutes.

◇ Scoop out the aubergine flesh with a spoon. Put it into a bowl with the meat mixture. Add the eggs and mix well. Season with pepper and a little salt. Put the aubergine skins into a greased ovenproof dish and fill each with this stuffing. Sprinkle with breadcrumbs and brown in the oven for 15 minutes.

INGREDIENTS

4 small aubergines (eggplants)
1 shallot
25 g (1 oz/2 tbsp) butter
100 g (4 oz) sausagemeat
250 g (9 oz) minced (ground) beef or lamb
2 eggs
salt and pepper
dried breadcrumbs

FIRST OR MAIN COURSE

SERVES 4–8
Preparation: 5 minutes
Cooking: 30 minutes
Difficulty: *
Cost: *

UTENSILS

1 bowl
1 very sharp knife
1 large sauté pan
1 baking tray
1 ovenproof dish
OVEN
200°C (400°F/Gas Mark 6)

◇ WARM SALAD OF AUBERGINES (EGGPLANTS) AND SWEETCORN ◇

This composed salad brings together vegetables whose different flavours and textures combine very pleasantly.

◇ Make the vinaigrette by mixing together all the ingredients and set aside.

◇ Skin and seed the tomatoes. Cut the flesh into small dice.

◇ Top and tail the French beans and soak them in cold water for 10 minutes.

◇ Bring a saucepan of salted water to the boil. Add the beans and cook briefly; they should still be crunchy. Plunge the beans into cold water, to prevent further cooking. Drain and leave to dry on a tea-towel.

◇ Cut the red pepper in half lengthways. Discard the stalk and seeds and cut the flesh into strips. Put the olive oil into a small saucepan, add the pepper strips and cover. Cook over a low heat until the pepper is tender. Remove the strips from the pan and drain on kitchen paper.

◇ If using fresh sweetcorn, cook it in boiling unsalted water for 5–10 minutes. Scrape the kernels from the cob when it is cool enough to handle. If using frozen sweetcorn, cook the kernels in boiling water for a few minutes until tender. If using canned sweetcorn, rinse and drain.

◇ Peel the aubergine and cut it into dice of just under 1 cm (½ inch). Heat the groundnut oil in a frying pan and fry the aubergine over a high heat, until coloured but not browned.

◇ Mix together all the vegetables except the aubergine in a serving dish. Add the vinaigrette and mix again. Scatter the still-warm aubergine on top. Serve immediately.

INGREDIENTS

2 medium tomatoes

300 g (10 oz) French (green) beans

1 red sweet pepper

10 ml (2 tsp) olive oil

1 medium corn on the cob, yielding
about 150 g (5 oz/about ⅔ cup)
(canned or frozen may be substituted)

1 aubergine (eggplant)

FOR THE VINAIGRETTE

10 ml (2 tsp) lemon juice

10 ml (2 tsp) wine vinegar

5 ml (1 tsp) sherry vinegar

20 ml (4 tsp) groundnut (peanut) oil

10 ml (2 tsp) olive oil

5 ml (1 tsp) prepared mustard

1 basil leaf, finely chopped

salt and pepper

FIRST COURSE

SERVES 4

Preparation: 30 minutes

Cooking: 25 minutes

Difficulty: ★★

Cost: ★

UTENSILS

2 saucepans

1 small sauté pan

1 frying pan

1 salad bowl

◇ BAKED AUBERGINE (EGGPLANT) WITH TUNA KEBABS ◇

◇ Wash the mushrooms and trim the stalks. Cut them in half. Cut the tuna into small cubes.

◇ Skin and seed the tomatoes. Cut the flesh of 2 of them into pieces the same size as the mushrooms; these will be used for the kebabs. Chop the rest of the tomato flesh into small dice.

◇ Peel and very finely chop the shallot. Sweat it gently in the butter in a sauté pan until transparent. Add the diced tomato and cook gently for 10 minutes. Remove from the heat and keep warm.

◇ Heat the oven to 200°C (400°F/Gas Mark 6).

◇ Bring a small saucepan of water to the boil. Blanch the unpeeled garlic for 5 minutes, then drain.

◇ Cut the aubergines in half lengthways. Put them cut side up on a baking tray; brush the cut surfaces with olive oil. Put the garlic on to the tray with the aubergine. Bake in the oven for 15–20 minutes, until the aubergines are tender.

◇ Meanwhile, prepare the tuna kebabs. Thread tuna, mushrooms and tomato alternately on to 4 small kebab skewers. Brush with olive oil. Cook the kebabs under a hot grill, turning and basting with the cooking juices, until cooked through. Keep warm.

◇ Remove the aubergine and garlic from the oven. Squeeze the pulp from each clove with a fork. Mash it and add it to the tomato mixture. Blend well.

◇ Coat the aubergine halves with the tomato and garlic mixture and top with a tuna kebab.

INGREDIENTS

200 g (7 oz) small mushrooms
1 fresh tuna steak, about 2 cm ($\frac{3}{4}$ inch)
thick, weighing about 450–550 g
(1–1$\frac{1}{4}$ lb)
450 g (1 lb) tomatoes
1 shallot
15 g ($\frac{1}{2}$ oz/1 tbsp) butter
6 garlic cloves, unpeeled
4 aubergines (eggplants)
olive oil

MAIN COURSE

SERVES 4
Preparation: 25 minutes
Cooking: 29 minutes
Difficulty: ★★
Cost: ★

UTENSILS

4 small kebab skewers
1 small saucepan
1 small sauté pan
1 baking tray
OVEN
200°C (400°F/Gas Mark 6)

◇ FRICASSEE OF AUBERGINES (EGGPLANT) WITH A COULIS OF RED PEPPERS ◇

This dish may also be enjoyed cold, as a summer dish. The pepper coulis should be chilled in the refrigerator, and the aubergine drained on kitchen paper after cooking. The dish is presented in the same manner.

◇ Heat the oven to 240°C (475°F/Gas Mark 9).
◇ Cut the red peppers in half lengthways. Discard the stalk and seeds. Cut the flesh into strips, then put into an ovenproof dish with the butter. Cook in the oven for 10 minutes. Add the cream and return to the oven for 5 minutes.
◇ Reduce the pepper mixture to a purée in a blender or food processor, then sieve, to make a smooth purée. Season with salt and pepper.
◇ Peel the aubergines. Cut them into dice of just under 1 cm (⅓ inch). Heat the olive oil in a frying pan and fry the aubergine over a high heat until coloured but not browned. Remove from the heat and season with salt and pepper.
◇ Pour a pool of the red pepper coulis on to each heated individual serving plate. Top with a cluster of aubergine dice and sprinkle with chervil.

INGREDIENTS

2 red sweet peppers
40 g (1½ oz/3 tbsp) butter
300 ml (10 fl oz/1¼ cups) double (heavy) cream
salt and pepper
2 aubergines (eggplants)
10 ml (2 tsp) olive oil
a little chervil

FIRST COURSE

SERVES 4
Preparation: 10 minutes
Cooking: 15 minutes
Difficulty: ★
Cost: ★

UTENSILS

1 ovenproof dish
1 blender or food processor
1 fine sieve
1 frying pan
OVEN
240°C (475°F/Gas Mark 9)

◇ FRIED AUBERGINES (EGGPLANTS) ◇

Slices of fried aubergine make an agreeable alternative to biscuits or nuts, when served with an apéritif.

◇ Peel the aubergines. Cut them into slices 5 mm (¼ inch) thick. Put them into a dish with a handful of salt and leave for 30 minutes, to degorge.
◇ Rinse the aubergine slices well. Drain them, then dry them in a tea-towel.
◇ Flour each slice lightly. Deep-fry them in oil, heated in a deep-fryer to 190°C (375°F), until golden-brown. Drain the slices on kitchen paper and sprinkle with salt.

INGREDIENTS

2 small aubergines (eggplants)
50 g (2 oz/6 tbsp) flour
coarse salt
oil for frying

COCKTAIL SNACK

SERVES 4–8
Preparation: 30 minutes
Cooking: 25 minutes
Difficulty: ★
Cost: ★

UTENSILS

1 deep-fryer
kitchen paper

◇ AUBERGINES (EGGPLANTS) WITH TOMATO AND TARRAGON ◇

◇ Heat the oven to 200°C (400°F/Gas Mark 6).

◇ Prick the aubergines all over. Put them on a baking tray and cook in the oven for 20–30 minutes, until tender. Cut the aubergines in half lengthways, taking care not to damage the skins.

◇ Meanwhile, skin and seed the tomatoes and cut the flesh into small dice.

◇ Peel and finely chop the shallot. Sweat the shallot gently in the butter in a sauté pan until transparent. Add the tomato and the bouquet garni. Season with salt and pepper and cook gently for about 10 minutes. The tomato mixture should retain its freshness and some of its texture. Do not crush it to a pulp.

◇ Remove the bouquet garni. Coat the aubergine halves with the tomato mixture and sprinkle with chopped tarragon. These are best eaten with a spoon.

INGREDIENTS

4 small aubergines (eggplants)
900 g (2 lb) ripe tomatoes
1 shallot
15 g (½oz/1 tbsp) butter
1 bouquet garni
salt and pepper
1 small bunch of fresh tarragon, chopped

FIRST COURSE

SERVES 4
Preparation: 5 minutes
Cooking: 20 minutes
Difficulty: ★
Cost: ★

UTENSILS

1 saucepan
1 sauté pan
1 baking tray
OVEN
200°C (400°F/Gas Mark 6)

◇ AUBERGINE (EGGPLANT) CURRY ◇

◇ Peel the aubergines and cut them into quarters. Peel the apples and slice thinly.

◇ Heat the oil in a saucepan. Add aubergines and apples. Cover and fry over a gentle heat for 15 minutes.

◇ Remove the aubergines and apples and drain well on kitchen paper.

◇ Stir the curry powder into the oil and juices in the pan and fry for 1–2 minutes. Add the cream and mix well. Return the vegetable mixture to the pan and allow to bubble over a moderate heat, so that the cream thickens into a smooth sauce. Serve immediately; this aubergine curry will not reheat well.

INGREDIENTS

450 g (1 lb) aubergines (eggplants)
2 dessert apples
50 ml (2 fl oz/3⅓ tbsp) groundnut (peanut) oil
10 ml (2 tsp) curry powder
300 ml (10 fl oz/1¼ cups) double (heavy) cream

SIDE DISH

SERVES 4
Preparation: 20 minutes
Cooking: 20 minutes
Difficulty: ★
Cost: ★

UTENSILS

1 medium saucepan
kitchen paper

S W E E T
◆ P E P P E R S ◆

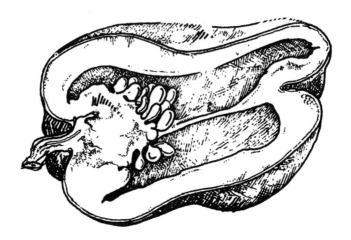

THE SWEET, OR bell, pepper is a member of the Capsicum family which has none of the fiery nature of its relative the chilli pepper. It was originally a native of Latin America, and was brought to Europe by Columbus. Like those other imports, the tomato and the aubergine, it has become very popular. Sweet peppers are rich in Vitamin C.

◇ BUYING SWEET PEPPERS ◇
Look for peppers with smooth, shiny, unmarked skins whose colour is bright and clear. Red, yellow or green varieties can be used, but most of the recipes in this section specify red peppers. However, there is no reason why you should not vary the colour of the fruit used.

◇ PREPARING SWEET PEPPERS ◇
It is essential to remove the skin and seeds. To do this, put the pepper under a hot grill (broiler) for a few minutes until black and blistered, or impale it on a fork and hold it over a gas flame, until charred. The skin can then be peeled off easily, and the pepper rinsed to remove any small charred bits of skin. Cut the pepper open lengthways and remove the seeds, unless you wish to use the pepper whole. In that case, cut away the stalk and use a spoon to remove the seeds. Rinse the pepper out, to ensure that all the seeds are removed.

◇ CHEF'S TIP ◇
Peppers freeze well, but their flavour may contaminate other foods if they are not carefully wrapped.

◇ CHILLED MUSSEL SOUP WITH RED PEPPERS ◇

◇ Peel and seed the peppers as described on page 20. Cut the peppers into small dice.

◇ Put the pepper into a small saucepan, add the olive oil and cook for about 10 minutes, partially covered. Remove the pepper with a slotted spoon and drain on kitchen paper. Chill in the refrigerator.

◇ Clean the mussels, scrubbing the shells if necessary. Put them into a large saucepan with the shallots, cream and plenty of pepper. Cook over a high heat until the mussel shells open (discard any that have not opened after a few minutes). Remove the mussels from the pan, reserving the creamy cooking liquid, and remove the shells. Cool, then chill the mussels in the refrigerator.

◇ Pass the creamy cooking liquid through a very fine sieve and chill in the refrigerator for several hours.

◇ Divide the mussels among 4 soup plates and sprinkle with a little chopped basil and some diced pepper. Spoon over the chilled creamy sauce.

INGREDIENTS

2 red sweet peppers
10 ml (2 tsp) olive oil
2 kg (4½ lb) mussels
2 shallots, peeled and chopped
150 ml (5 fl oz/⅔ cup) double (heavy) cream
basil leaves

FIRST COURSE

SERVES 4
Preparation: 20 minutes + 2 hours chilling
Cooking: 5–10 minutes
Difficulty: ★
Cost: ★

UTENSILS

1 large saucepan
1 small saucepan
kitchen paper
1 fine sieve

◇ PORK TENDERLOIN WITH RED PEPPERS ◇

Serve this with a green vegetable, such as broccoli or French beans.

◇ Peel and seed the pepper, as described on page 20, and cut into strips.

◇ Put the pepper strips into a small saucepan with the olive oil and cook gently for about 10 minutes, until soft. Reduce the pepper to a purée in a blender or food processor, then sieve to make a very smooth purée.

◇ Cut the pork tenderloin into slices about 2 cm (¾ inch) thick and season with salt and pepper. Melt the butter in a frying pan and fry the pork for 3–4 minutes: the meat should not be cooked long enough to make it harden. Remove the pork from the pan and keep warm.

◇ Peel and finely chop the shallot and add to the butter remaining in the pan. Cook gently until transparent, but not coloured. Add the cream to the pan and boil until it thickens. Stir in 5 ml (1 tsp) of the pepper purée and a dash of lemon juice. Check the seasoning.

◇ Arrange the pork slices on heated dinner plates and coat them with the pepper sauce. Serve immediately.

INGREDIENTS

1 red sweet pepper
10 ml (2 tsp) olive oil
700 g (1½ lb) pork tenderloin
50 g (2 oz/4 tbsp) butter
1 shallot
200 ml (7 fl oz/⅞ cup) double cream
a little lemon juice

MAIN COURSE

SERVES 4
Preparation: 10 minutes
Cooking: 20 minutes
Difficulty: ★★
Cost: ★★

UTENSILS

1 small saucepan
1 blender or food processor
1 fine sieve
1 large frying pan

◇ MEDALLIONS OF MONKFISH WITH MANGE-TOUT (SNOW PEAS) AND RED PEPPER BUTTER ◇

◇ Clean the stock vegetables and chop them coarsely. Place in a saucepan with the herbs and 600 ml (1 pint/2½ cups) water. Bring to the boil, then simmer for 20 minutes.

◇ Peel and seed the peppers as described on page 20.

◇ Put the pieces of pepper into a saucepan with a lid, add the olive oil and cook, covered, for about 10 minutes, until soft. Remove with a slotted spoon and reduce to a purée in a blender or food processor.

◇ To make the beurre blanc sauce, peel and very finely chop the shallots. Put the shallots, vinegar, white wine and a pinch of salt into a small saucepan. Place over a brisk heat until the liquid has almost entirely evaporated.

◇ Add the cream and allow to reduce. Lower the heat and whisk in the butter a little at a time, until creamy. Add 10 ml (2 tsp) of the pepper purée and mix well. Season to taste with salt and pepper, then sieve. Set aside.

◇ Bring the stock to the boil in a large saucepan and poach the monkfish medallions gently for 4–5 minutes (the stock should barely simmer). Remove the monkfish with a slotted spoon, drain on kitchen paper and keep warm.

◇ Top and tail the mange-tout. Bring a saucepan of salted water to the boil and cook the mange-touts for 2–3 minutes. Drain and fry gently in the butter for 1 minute (do not allow the mange-tout to colour).

◇ Place 3 or 4 monkfish medallions on each heated dinner plate. Coat with the pepper butter sauce and surround with a border of mange-tout.

INGREDIENTS

150 g (5 oz) red sweet peppers
10 ml (2 tsp) olive oil
550 g (1¼ lb) monkfish, cut into medallions about 1 cm (½ inch) thick
450 g (1 lb) mange-tout (snow peas)
15 g (½ oz/1 tbsp) butter

FOR THE STOCK
1 celery stalk
1 carrot
1 onion
1 small bunch of parsley
1 thyme sprig
½ bay leaf
100 ml (4 fl oz/½ cup) dry white wine

FOR THE BEURRE
BLANC SAUCE
2 shallots
50 ml (2 fl oz/¼ cup) sherry vinegar
50 ml (2 fl oz/¼ cup) dry white wine
salt
20 ml (2 tbsp) double (heavy) cream
200 g (7 oz/1¾ sticks) butter, softened

MAIN COURSE

SERVES 4
Preparation: 15 minutes
Cooking: 30 minutes
Difficulty: ★★
Cost: ★★

UTENSILS

1 large saucepan
1 medium saucepan
1 small saucepan
1 blender or food processor
1 small balloon whisk
1 fine sieve
1 frying pan

◇ RED PEPPER AND FENNEL RAMEKINS WITH A TOMATO COULIS ◇

◇ Clean and chop the stock vegetables. Put them into a saucepan with the herbs and 250 ml (9 fl oz/1⅛ cups) water. Bring to the boil, then simmer for about 20 minutes. Strain and allow to cool.

◇ Peel and seed the peppers as described on page 20, then cut the peppers into strips.

◇ Put the pepper strips into a saucepan with 30 ml (2 tbsp) of the olive oil and cook, partially covered, until soft. Reduce the pepper to a purée in a blender or food processor, then sieve to make a very smooth purée.

◇ Cut the fennel into 1 cm (½ inch) dice. Melt 25 g (1 oz/2 tbsp) of the butter in a saucepan and add the fennel and 100 ml (4 fl oz/½ cup) water. Season with salt. Cook, uncovered, for about 12–15 minutes, until the fennel is tender and lightly glazed.

◇ Heat the oven to 170°C (325°F/Gas Mark 3).

◇ Mix the cream with the egg yolks, season with salt and pepper and add 45 ml (3 tbsp) of the pepper purée. Spoon the mixture into 4 individual buttered ramekins and top each with 5 ml (1 tsp) diced fennel. Bake for 20–25 minutes, then unmould on to individual serving plates and allow to cool.

◇ Skin and seed the tomato. Reduce to a purée in a blender or food processor with 100 ml (4 fl oz/½ cup) of the stock, the remaining olive oil and the lemon juice. Season with salt and pepper. Use to coat the vegetable moulds.

INGREDIENTS

2 large red sweet peppers
150 ml (5 fl oz/⅔ cup) olive oil
2 fennel bulbs
100 g (4 oz/1 stick) butter
salt
150 ml (5 fl oz/⅔ cup) double (heavy) cream
2 egg yolks
pepper
1 tomato
juice of ½ lemon

FOR THE VEGETABLE STOCK
1 onion
1 shallot
1 small leek
1 carrot
1 celery stalk
1 thyme sprig
1 bay leaf
1 parsley sprig

FIRST COURSE

SERVES 4
Preparation: 15 minutes
Cooking: 40 minutes
Difficulty: **
Cost: *

UTENSILS

2 saucepans
1 blender or food processor
1 fine sieve
1 small basin
4 ramekins
OVEN
170°C (325°F/Gas Mark 3)

◇ Clean and chop the stock vegetables. Put them into a saucepan with the herbs and 600 ml (1 pint/2½ cups) water. Bring to the boil, then simmer for about 20 minutes. Strain and leave to cool.

◇ Peel and slice the onions, scrape and slice the carrots. Skin and seed the tomato; dice the flesh. Cut the lamb into chunks about 4cm (1½ inches) square. Heat 10 ml (2 tsp) of the olive oil and the butter in a large sauté pan with a lid. Fry the lamb over a brisk heat until well coloured.

◇ Remove the lamb from the pan and set aside. Add the onion and carrot to the pan and fry until they begin to colour, then add the garlic, the bouquet garni and tomato. Season with salt and pepper and add about 450 ml (¾ pint/2 cups) of the stock, to just cover the meat. Cover and leave to simmer for 1 hour.

◇ Peel and seed the pepper as described on page 20, then cut into strips. Put the pepper strips into a small saucepan with the remaining olive oil, and cook, partially covered, for about 10 minutes, until soft. Reduce the pepper to a purée in a blender or food processor, then sieve to make a very smooth purée.

◇ When the lamb is cooked, strain off and reserve the cooking liquid and discard the garlic and bouquet garni. Keep the lamb warm.

◇ Purée the cooking liquid in a blender or food processor, then sieve and add the pepper purée. Mix well. Check the seasoning. Return the sauce to the pan with the lamb and reheat gently. Serve very hot.

INGREDIENTS

50 g (2 oz) onions
50 g (2 oz) carrots
1 tomato
400 g (14 oz) shoulder of lamb
400 g (14 oz) neck of lamb
20 ml (4 tsp) olive oil
25 g (1 oz/2 tbsp) butter
½ bulb of garlic
1 bouquet garni
salt and pepper
1 red or green sweet pepper

FOR THE VEGETABLE STOCK
1 onion
2 shallots
1 leek
2 carrots
1 stalk celery
1 thyme sprig
1 bay leaf
1 parsley sprig

MAIN COURSE

SERVES 4
Preparation: 10 minutes
Cooking: 1 hour
Difficulty: ★★
Cost: ★★

UTENSILS

1 large sauté pan with a lid
1 small saucepan
1 blender or food processor
1 fine sieve

This recipe allows for the preparation of a large quantity of chicken stock, which may be frozen for future use.

◇ Clean and chop the stock vegetables. Place in a large saucepan with the chicken carcasses, herbs, salt, peppercorns, wine and 2 litres (3½ pints/2 quarts) water. Bring to the boil, then simmer for 20 minutes.

◇ Place the stock in the base of a steamer and keep just below boiling point.

◇ Rub the chicken all over with the cut lemon, to prevent it from discolouring during cooking. Season inside and out with salt and pepper. Place the chicken in the upper part of the steamer and cover. Steam, keeping the liquid at a simmer, for about 1½ hours, until the chicken is tender and cooked through.

◇ Meanwhile, peel and seed the pepper as described on page 20, then cut into strips.

◇ Put the pepper strips into a small saucepan with the olive oil and cook, partially covered, for 10 minutes, until soft. Reduce the pepper to a purée in a blender or food processor, then sieve to make a very smooth purée.

◇ Peel and finely chop the shallot. Place in a blender or food processor with the juice of the remaining lemon, the groundnut and hazelnut oils, vinegars, salt and pepper, 250 ml (9 fl oz/1⅛ cups) of the chicken stock and 10 ml (2 tsp) pepper purée. Blend until smooth.

◇ Steam the cauliflower florets for the garnish until they are just tender.

◇ Carve the chicken. Spoon a pool of sweet pepper sauce on to each dinner plate and place a serving of chicken on top. Arrange a few cauliflower florets and chives around the chicken.

INGREDIENTS

1 chicken, about 1.6 kg (3½ lb)
1½ lemons
salt and pepper
1 red sweet pepper
10 ml (2 tsp) olive oil
1 shallot
45 ml (3 tbsp) groundnut (peanut) oil
5 ml (1 tsp) hazelnut oil
20 ml (4 tsp) wine vinegar
20 ml (4 tsp) sherry vinegar
FOR THE CHICKEN STOCK
100 g (4 oz) mushrooms
1 onion
1 celery stalk
1 leek
100 g (4 oz) carrots
900 g (2 lb) chicken carcasses (about 2–3 carcasses)
3 garlic cloves, unpeeled
1 thyme sprig
¼ bay leaf
3 parsley stalks
salt
a few crushed black peppercorns
100 ml (4 fl oz/½ cup) dry white wine
TO GARNISH
1 small cauliflower, broken into florets
a few chopped chives

MAIN COURSE

SERVES 4
Preparation: 30 minutes
Cooking: 2 hours
Difficulty: ★★
Cost: ★★

UTENSILS

1 steamer
1 large saucepan
1 small saucepan
1 blender or food processor
1 fine sieve

•T O M A T O E S•

THE TOMATO, BROUGHT to Europe in the sixteenth century by the conquistadores, was originally a native of Peru and Mexico. Although it was quickly accepted in southerm Europe, particular in Italy and Spain, the inhabitants of northern Europe were much more cautious in their reaction; after all, the tomato is a relative of such poisonous plants as belladonna and the mandrake. Not until 1778 was the tomato listed as an edible plant in France, and the British took even longer to adopt the newcomer. The tomato craves warmth if it is to grow well, but sunshine is also of paramount importance if its flavour is to develop fully. Late summer tomatoes, ripened naturally in the sun, are the best of all.

Tomatoes are rich in Vitamins A and C, together with potassium. They also contain citrates, tartrates and oxalates, which are principally responsible for their flavour. Due to their oxalic acid content, they should be avoided by those who suffer from rheumatism.

◇ BUYING TOMATOES ◇

Always look for well-ripened tomatoes, whatever the recipe you have in mind. Fresh tomatoes should feel firm to the touch, with a smooth, taut, unblemished skin. End of season tomatoes are likely to have the fullest flavour.

Green tomatoes are difficult to digest. To hasten ripening, wrap individual tomatoes in newspaper and place them in a cool, dark place.

◇ SERVING TOMATOES ◇

Tomatoes may be served with an enormous variety of other foods. They can be used in first course salads or soups; they can make a main dish in their own right, if stuffed with meat or fish. Tomato coulis is a delicious accompaniment to many different types of meat, fish or vegetable dishes; tomatoes are an essential flavouring in many sauces, stews, etc.

◇ PREPARING TOMATOES ◇

Unless tomatoes are to be left whole and stuffed, or used as a garnish, the most usual way of preparing them is as follows:

◇ Cut away a small cone of flesh immediately below the stalk; this removes the hard inner core.

◇ Skin the tomatoes by immersing them briefly in boiling water, then in iced water. Cutting a small cross at the base may speed up this operation.

◇ Slice the tomato in half horizontally and remove the seeds.

◇ Chop the tomatoes as required.

◇ CHEF'S TIPS ◇

To keep tomatoes at their best during storage, make sure that they are standing on their base and are not touching each other.

Tomatoes should be skinned and seeded before freezing. Tomato coulis, soups, etc. freeze very well indeed.

◇ TOMATO SOUP WITH PEAS AND GARLIC ◇

◇ Cut the tomatoes in half horizontally and remove the seeds and juice. Reduce the flesh to a purée in a blender or food processor. Put it into a saucepan with the butter, the bouquet garni herbs tied together, the sugar, salt and pepper. Simmer gently for 20 minutes, then discard the bouquet garni.

◇ Cook the peas in a little boiling salted water until just tender, then drain.

◇ Meanwhile, plunge the garlic into boiling water for 30 seconds, then peel. Cook the garlic in boiling water until very soft.

◇ Pour 1–2 ladlefuls very hot tomato soup into each heated soup plate. Place a garlic clove in the centre of each and scatter over a few peas. Serve immediately.

INGREDIENTS

550 g (1¼ lb) tomatoes
25 g (1 oz/2 tbsp) butter
a pinch of sugar
salt and pepper
50 g (2 oz) peas (shelled weight)
4 garlic cloves
BOUQUET GARNI
1 parsley sprig
1 thyme sprig
¼ bay leaf
1 rosemary sprig
1 tarragon sprig
1 celery stalk

FIRST COURSE

SERVES 4
Preparation: under 5 minutes
Cooking: 25 minutes
Difficulty: ★★
Cost: ★

UTENSILS

1 blender or food processor
fine string
2 small saucepans
1 large saucepan
1 frying pan

◇ TOMATO COULIS WITH BASIL ◇

◇ Skin and seed the tomatoes as described on page 27. Reduce the flesh to a purée in a blender or food processor and add the basil.

◇ Put the tomato purée into a saucepan and heat. As soon as it starts to bubble, remove the pan from the heat. Sieve the purée to remove the basil.

INGREDIENTS

900 g (2 lb) tomatoes
1 basil leaf

SAUCE

Preparation: 5–15 minutes
Cooking: 5 minutes
Difficulty: ★
Cost: ★

UTENSILS

1 saucepan
1 blender or food processor
1 sieve

◇ BAKED TOMATOES ◇

◇ Heat the oven to 200°C (400°F/Gas Mark 6).

◇ Cut the tomatoes in half horizontally. Arrange them, cut side upwards, in an ovenproof dish. Sprinkle with the oil and season with salt and pepper. Bake for 7–8 minutes.

◇ Meanwhile, chop the parsley and peeled garlic finely. Mix 45 ml (3 tbsp) of the parsley with the breadcrumbs and garlic.

◇ Remove the tomatoes from the oven and sprinkle them with the breadcrumb mixture. Brown them under a hot grill or in the oven, taking care that the crumb topping does not overbrown.

INGREDIENTS

550 g (1¼ lb) tomatoes
45 ml (3 tbsp) olive oil
salt and pepper
1 bunch of parsley
1 garlic clove
45 ml (3 tbsp) dried breadcrumbs

SIDE DISH

SERVES 4
Preparation: under 5 minutes
Cooking: 5–15 minutes
Difficulty: ★
Cost: ★

UTENSILS

1 ovenproof dish
1 bowl
1 chopping board
OVEN
200°C (400°F/Gas Mark 6)

If the tart is served cold, accompany it with a chive-flavoured cream; omit this if it is served warm.

◇ Cut the tomatoes in half horizontally and remove the seeds and juice. Lay the tomato halves flat and slice them horizontally into rounds. As you work, lay the sliced tomatoes on kitchen paper, to soak up as much liquid as possible. Then turn all the slices over and lay them on fresh sheets of paper.

◇ Purée the basil and oil in a blender or food processor.

◇ Heat the oven to 220°C (425°F/Gas Mark 7).

◇ Roll out the pastry 2 mm ($\frac{1}{8}$ inch) thick and use to line a 9 inch (23 cm) flan tin (tart pan/pie plate). Brush the pastry with the oil. Arrange the tomato rounds in the flan and brush them with the basil oil. Season with salt and pepper. Bake for 15 minutes.

◇ If serving the flan cold, peel and finely chop the shallot and chop the chives. Mix into the cream with the lemon juice, salt and pepper. Serve in a sauceboat.

INGREDIENTS

450 g (1 lb) tomatoes
1 bunch of basil
100 ml (4 fl oz/$\frac{1}{2}$ cup) olive oil
200 g (7 oz) flaky (puff) pastry
salt and pepper
FOR THE CHIVE-FLAVOURED CREAM
1 shallot
a few chives
150 ml (5 fl oz/$\frac{2}{3}$ cup) double (heavy) cream
juice of $\frac{1}{2}$ lemon
salt and pepper

FIRST COURSE

SERVES 4
Preparation: 5–15 minutes
Cooking: 20–35 minutes
Difficulty: ★★
Cost: ★

UTENSILS

1 flan tin (tart pan/pie plate)
1 blender or food processor
kitchen paper
OVEN
220°C (425°F/Gas Mark 7)

◇ BAKED TOMATOES, COURGETTES (ZUCCHINI) AND AUBERGINES (EGGPLANTS) ◇

As far as possible, use vegetables which, when sliced, are of the same diameter.

◇ Peel the aubergines and cut them into 5 mm (¼ inch) slices. Wash and trim the courgettes and cut them into slices of the same thickness.

◇ Cut the tomatoes into 2 mm (⅛ inch) slices.

◇ Heat the oven to 180°C (350°F/Gas Mark 4).

◇ Grease the dish generously with the butter. Arrange a layer of tomato slices in the dish, then a layer of courgettes, then another layer of tomato, and finally a layer of aubergine. Repeat the layers until all the tomato, courgette and aubergine slices are used up.

◇ Season with salt and pepper and sprinkle with the oil. Bake for 1½ hours.

INGREDIENTS

200 g (7 oz) aubergines (eggplants)
150 g (5 oz) courgettes (zucchini)
200 g (7 oz) tomatoes
50 g (2 oz/4 tbsp) butter
salt and pepper
45 ml (3 tbsp) olive oil

FIRST COURSE OR SIDE DISH

SERVES 4
Preparation: 5–15 minutes
Cooking: 1½ hours
Difficulty: *
Cost: *

UTENSILS

1 ovenproof dish
OVEN
180°C (350°F/Gas Mark 4)

◇ TOMATOES FLAMBEED IN PASTIS, WITH FENNEL ◇

◇ Reduce 300 g (10 oz) of the tomatoes to a purée in a blender or food processor, then sieve, pressing hard with the back of a spoon to extract as much of the pulp as possible.

◇ Heat the oven to 180°C (350°F/Gas Mark 4).

◇ Cut the remaining tomatoes in half horizontally, arrange them in an ovenproof dish and sprinkle with 10 ml (2 tsp) of the olive oil. Bake in the oven for 7–8 minutes.

◇ Meanwhile, wash the fennel and slice it into 1 cm (½ inch) strips. Heat the remaining oil in a sauté pan with a lid and cook the fennel gently. When it is half cooked, add the tomato purée and continue cooking until the fennel strips are tender.

◇ Remove the tomatoes from the oven; pour the pastis over the tomatoes and flame it. Tilt the dish and baste the tomatoes with the liquid. Return the dish to the oven for 2 minutes.

◇ Arrange the fennel on a heated serving dish and top with the tomatoes.

INGREDIENTS

700 g (1½ lb) small tomatoes
30 ml (2 tbsp) olive oil
200 g (7 oz) fennel
100 ml (4 fl oz/½ cup) pastis

FIRST COURSE

Preparation: under 5 minutes
Cooking: 5–15 minutes
Difficulty: *
Cost: *

UTENSILS

1 blender or food processor
1 sieve
1 ovenproof dish
1 sauté pan with a lid
OVEN
180°C (350°F/Gas Mark 4)

◇ SAUTEED MUSSELS WITH CHILLED TOMATO SAUCE ◇

◇ Reduce the tomatoes to a purée in a blender or food processor. Sieve the purée to extract the skin and seeds, then chill the purée in the refrigerator.

◇ Wash and scrub the mussels. Place them in a large saucepan and heat briskly, shaking the pan frequently, until all the shells are open. Discard any that do not open promptly. Cool and shell the mussels.

◇ Just before serving, pour the chilled tomato sauce onto individual serving plates.

◇ Heat the butter in a large sauté pan until it begins to brown. Fry the mussels rapidly for 10–15 seconds. It is important that the mussels fry briskly; cook them in batches if the temperature of the pan falls.

◇ Place mussels on a heated serving dish and serve immediately, so that the contrast between the hot mussels and the chilled sauce can be appreciated to the full.

INGREDIENTS

200 g (7 oz) tomatoes
900 g (2 lb) mussels
50 g (2 oz/2 tbsp) butter

FIRST COURSE

SERVES 4
Preparation: 15–30 minutes
Cooking: under 5 minutes
Difficulty: ★★
Cost: ★

UTENSILS

1 blender or food processor
1 sieve
1 large saucepan
1 large frying pan

◇ FRESH TOMATO SAUCE ◇

◇ Skin and seed the tomatoes as described on page 27. Chop the flesh roughly.

◇ Peel and finely chop the onion and garlic. Heat the olive oil in a large saucepan and cook the onion and garlic gently until the onion begins to become transparent. Then add the tomatoes, herbs, salt and pepper. Cook very gently for 1 hour, stirring frequently.

INGREDIENTS

900 g (2 lb) tomatoes
1 onion
3 garlic cloves
10 ml (2 tsp) olive oil
basil or tarragon (optional)
3 parsley stalks
1 small thyme sprig
½ bay leaf
salt and pepper

SAUCE

Preparation: 5–15 minutes
Cooking: 1 hour
Difficulty: ★
Cost: ★

UTENSILS

1 large saucepan
1 small sharp knife

◇ Arrange the cherry tomatoes for the garnish in a single layer in a sauté pan with a lid. Add 30 ml (2 tbsp) water and the butter, cover and cook over a very gentle heat for 15 minutes.

◇ Meanwhile, place the fish trimmings in a saucepan with the parsley, onion and 350 ml (12 fl oz/1½ cups) water. Bring to the boil, then simmer for 10 minutes.

◇ Skin and seed the large tomatoes. Chop the flesh into 5 mm (¼ inch) dice. Peel and finely chop the shallots.

◇ Heat the oven to 180°C (350°F/Gas Mark 4). Grease an ovenproof dish generously with the butter. Arrange the diced tomato and chopped shallot in the dish. Add 200 ml (7 fl oz/⅞ cup) of the stock.

◇ Arrange the fish fillets in the dish; add the chopped parsley, season with salt and pepper and cover with kitchen foil. Bake for 10–15 minutes until the liquid begins to simmer, then cook for a further 5 minutes and remove from the oven. Transfer the fish fillets to a heated serving dish and keep warm.

◇ Tip the contents of the baking dish into a sauté pan and reduce until it begins to thicken. Add the cream, return to the boil and allow to reduce for 3 minutes. Season to taste with salt, pepper and lemon juice.

◇ Coat the fish fillets with the cream sauce and surround with the small cooked tomatoes. Sprinkle with a little chopped parsley. Serve immediately.

INGREDIENTS

4 large tomatoes

3 shallots

75 g (3 oz/6 tbsp) butter

550 g (1¼ lb) brill fillets (or other flat fish)

1 small bunch of parsley, chopped

salt and pepper

150 ml (5 fl oz/⅔ cup) double (heavy) cream

juice of 1 lemon

TO GARNISH

250 g (9 oz) cherry tomatoes

15 g (½ oz/1 tbsp) butter

fish trimmings

FOR THE FISH STOCK

1 small bunch of parsley

1 onion, peeled and sliced

MAIN COURSE

Preparation: 5–15 minutes

Cooking: 15–30 minutes

Difficulty: ★★

Cost: ★★

UTENSILS

1 sauté pan with a lid

1 chopping board

2 saucepans

1 ovenproof dish

kitchen foil

OVEN

180°C (350°F/Gas Mark 4)

◆COURGETTES◆

ZUCCHINI

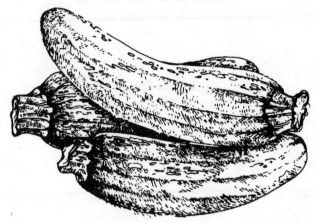

COURGETTES (ZUCCHINI), WHICH are baby marrows (squash), have the same origins and properties as their big brothers. The marrow originated in India, and has long been cultivated in warm and temperate areas of the globe. The French enjoy courgettes; the Italians delight in them. But only after World War II, and then slowly, did they become familiar to the British.

Courgettes have a high water content of 90 per cent; however, they do provide valuable amounts of potassium and Vitamins A (mostly in the skin), C and folic acid. Like aubergines (eggplants), courgettes absorb fat readily.

Unless you grow your own courgettes, you are most unlikely to be able to obtain specific varieties.

◇ BUYING COURGETTES ◇

A good courgette weighs heavy in the hand. The stalk should be firmly attached, the skin smooth and unblemished.

◇ PREPARING COURGETTES ◇

Wash and dry the courgettes. Trim the stalk and flower ends. If the courgettes are sufficiently young and tender, they will not need to be peeled.

For most recipes, courgettes are sliced into rounds. If they are to be stuffed, halve lengthways. Spoon out seeds and flesh, leaving at least 1 cm ($\frac{1}{2}$ inch) flesh on each side and a little more at the base. Do not pierce the skin.

◇ COOKING COURGETTES ◇

Sauté the sliced courgettes in oil or butter. Or blanch them in boiling water for 2 minutes, then stuff and bake for 8–10 minutes.

◇ CHEF'S TIP ◇

An attractive decorative effect may be obtained if courgettes are peeled with a potato peeler, to leave alternate stripes of green skin and white flesh.

◇ COURGETTE (ZUCCHINI) AND HAM GRATIN ◇

◇ Skin and seed the tomatoes; dice the flesh. Peel and finely chop the shallot.

◇ Wash and trim the courgettes. Halve them lengthways. Chop the ham coarsely.

◇ Melt half the butter in a gratin dish over a gentle heat and sweat the shallot until transparent. Add the tomato and cook for 5 minutes.

◇ Meanwhile, melt the remaining butter in a frying pan. Fry the courgettes over a brisk heat for 5 minutes.

◇ Put the cream into a small saucepan, bring to the boil and remove it from the heat. Heat the oven to 180°C (350°F/Gas Mark 4).

◇ Arrange a layer of courgettes in the gratin dish on top of the tomatoes. Season with salt and pepper. Spread the chopped ham over them in an even layer. Top with the remaining courgettes. Coat with the cream and cook in the oven for 30 minutes.

INGREDIENTS

2 tomatoes

1 shallot

550 g (1¼ lb) courgettes (zucchini)

250 g (9 oz) cooked ham

25 g (1 oz/2tbsp) butter

150 ml (5 fl oz/⅔ cup) double (heavy) cream

salt and pepper

MAIN COURSE

SERVES 4

Preparation: 10 minutes

Cooking: 40 minutes

Difficulty: ★

Cost: ★

UTENSILS

1 small saucepan

1 flameproof gratin dish

1 frying pan

OVEN

180°C (350°F/Gas Mark 4)

◇ COURGETTES (ZUCCHINI) MEUNIERE ◇

◇ Wash and trim the courgettes. Slice them lengthways into a fan shape, cutting to within 2 cm (¾ inch) of the stalk end, to hold the slices together.

◇ Open out the fan. Sprinkle with salt and pepper. Dip the courgette fans into flour and shake off any excess.

◇ Heat the butter until it begins to brown. Fry the courgette fans for 5 minutes on each side.

INGREDIENTS

4 small courgettes (zucchini)

salt and pepper

a little flour

20 g (¾ oz/1½ tbsp) butter

SIDE DISH

SERVES 4

Preparation: 5–10 minutes

Cooking: 5–10 minutes

Difficulty: ★

Cost: ★

UTENSILS

1 large frying pan

◇ COURGETTE (ZUCCHINI) FRITTERS ◇

Serve hot with grilled meat, or warm as an apéritif snack.

◇ To make the batter, pre-heat a mixing bowl by standing it in a larger bowl of boiling water.
◇ Put the yeast, salt and 5 ml (1 tsp) warm water into the warmed bowl. When the yeast and salt are dissolved, add the oil and flour. Work the mixture well with your fingers. Cover and leave to stand for 2 hours in a warm place.
◇ Wash and trim the courgettes. Cut them into slices 2 mm (⅛ inch) thick.
◇ Heat oil in a deep-fryer to 190°C (375°F).
◇ When ready to use the batter, beat the egg white stiffly and fold into the batter mixture. Coat the courgette slices in batter and lower into the hot oil. Fry until golden brown, then remove and drain on kitchen paper. Sprinkle with salt.

INGREDIENTS

300 g (10 oz) small courgettes (zucchini)
oil for deep-frying
FOR THE BATTER
2–3 g (⅛ oz) fresh yeast or ⅔ tsp dried
a pinch of salt
10 ml (2 tsp) olive oil
50 g (2 oz/6 tbsp) plain (all-purpose) flour
1 egg white

SIDE DISH/COCKTAIL SNACK

SERVES 4
Resting for batter: 2 hours
Preparation: 10 minutes
Cooking: 5 minutes
Difficulty: ★
Cost: ★

UTENSILS

1 mixing bowl
1 deep-fryer
kitchen paper

◇ COURGETTES (ZUCCHINI) SAUTEED IN OLIVE OIL ◇

◇ Wash and trim the courgettes. Slice them into 1 cm (½ inch) rounds. Sauté the slices in the olive oil in a frying pan, allowing them to become nicely browned on each side.
◇ Season with salt and pepper and sprinkle with chopped parsley or basil.

INGREDIENTS

450 g (1 lb) small courgettes (zucchini)
50 ml (2 fl oz/scant ¼ cup) olive oil
continental parsley or basil leaves
salt and pepper

SIDE DISH

SERVES 4
Preparation: 5 minues
Cooking: 5 minutes
Difficulty: ★
Cost: ★

UTENSILS

1 large frying pan

$\bullet$ C U C U M B E R S $\bullet$

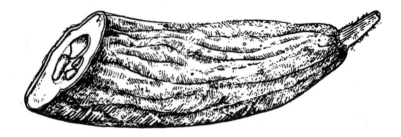

How the cucumber, which originally grew wild in the Himalayan foothills some 6,000 years ago, migrated to Egypt, is unknown. But we do know that the cucumber became one of the favourite dishes of the Pharaohs, and that when expelled from Egypt the Hebrews took cucumbers with them to the Promised Land. Even today, cucumber often features on Israeli breakfast menus. In ancient Rome, the Emperor Tiberius adored cucumbers. During his reign, the most celebrated Roman gastronome, Apicius, invented a recipe including boiled cucumber, brains, honey, cumin, celery seeds, oil and eggs.

There are many varieties of cucumber, and it can be bought throughout the year. Surprisingly, given their high water content, gardeners find that cucumbers do better in dry conditions, since an excess of wet weather makes them bitter.

The cucumber is low in calories, containing neither oils nor sugars; despite this, it can be difficult to digest. However, the many women who use cucumbers in beauty preparations will overlook this. Cucumber juice, rich in sulphur, tightens dilated pores; the ladies of ancient Rome spent hours applying layers of cucumber slices to their faces.

$\diamond$ BUYING CUCUMBER $\diamond$

Look for firm, smooth, plump specimens. Smaller cucumbers tend to have fewer seeds. Allow 100–150 g (4–5 oz) per person.

$\diamond$ PREPARING CUCUMBER $\diamond$

Peel the cucumber (some people find the skin particularly indigestible) and, if necessary, remove the seeds. When served raw, cucumbers exude large quantities of water. Accelerate this by slicing the cucumber into rounds and sprinkling them with salt. Leave the slices to drain in a colander for about 30 minutes. Then rinse and press gently to extract as much water as possible.

◇ COOKING AND SERVING CUCUMBER ◇

Cucumber is equally appetizing served hot or cold. Cold, it may form part of many different salads and hors d'oeuvres. As a hot vegetable, it is particularly good with fish and, stuffed with meat or fish, it makes an excellent main course.

When serving hot, blanch the cucumber pieces in boiling salted water; cook for about 10 minutes after the water has returned to the boil. Drain the cucumber, serve with melted butter and chopped parsley, or coated with sauce.

Cucumber may also be steamed or fried.

◇ LANGOUSTINES WITH GLAZED CUCUMBER ◇

◇ Separate the langoustine tails from the bodies. Peel away the shells. Reserve the tails and discard the remainder.

◇ Peel the cucumber. Cut it in half lengthways and remove the seeds. Cut the cucumber flesh into sticks 2 cm ($\frac{3}{4}$ inch) wide, and 1 cm ($\frac{1}{2}$ inch) shorter than the langoustine tails.

◇ Put the cucumber sticks into a sauté pan with 25 g (1 oz/2 tbsp) of the butter and a pinch of salt. Add enough water to come halfway up the cucumber. Cook over a gentle heat until the water has completely evaporated, turning the cucumber gently from time to time, so that it is completely coated in butter. By the end of the cooking time, the cucumber should be brilliantly shiny.

◇ Melt the remaining butter in another sauté pan and allow it to brown slightly. Fry the langoustine tails for 1 minute on each side. Remove from the pan and keep warm. Add the lemon juice and salt and pepper to taste to the juices in the pan and mix well.

◇ Arrange the langoustines and cucumber on heated dinner plates. Spoon a little of the cooking juices in the pan over each plate.

INGREDIENTS

16–24 langoustines (or Pacific prawns)
1 cucumber
75 g (3 oz/6 tbsp) butter
salt
juice of $\frac{1}{2}$ lemon
pepper

MAIN COURSE

SERVES 4
Preparation: 5 minutes
Cooking: 10 minutes
Difficulty: ★★
Cost: ★★★

UTENSILS

2 sauté pans

◇ Skin and seed one of the tomatoes; cut the flesh into small dice.

◇ Chop the tuna coarsely. Chop the parsley. Peel and chop the shallot finely.

◇ Heat the oven to 180°C (350°F/Gas Mark 4). Melt 15 g (¼ oz/1 tbsp) of the butter in a sauté pan. Cook the shallot gently until it is transparent. Add the tuna and diced tomato and cook for 5 minutes. Remove the pan from the heat. Add the parsley and salt and pepper to taste. Mix well. Check the seasoning.

◇ Peel the cucumbers. Cut them in half lengthways and remove the seeds. Stuff the cucumbers with the tuna mixture. Place them in an oiled ovenproof dish and bake in the oven for 15 minutes.

◇ While the cucumber is cooling, prepare a tomato purée. Chop the remaining tomatoes coarsely. Place them in a small saucepan with the garlic and bouquet garni. Cook over a medium heat for 15 minutes. Season to taste with salt and pepper. Reduce to a purée in a food processor or blender, then sieve to make a smooth purée. Add the remaining butter and mix well.

◇ Pour a pool of tomato purée on to each heated dinner plate. Place a half stuffed cucumber on each plate.

INGREDIENTS

3 tomatoes
550 g (1¼ lb) fresh tuna
1 bunch of parsley
1 shallot
40 g (1½ oz/3 tbsp) butter
salt and pepper
2 cucumbers
1 garlic clove
1 bouquet garni

MAIN COURSE

SERVES 4
Preparation: 10 minutes
Cooking: 20 minutes
Difficulty: ★★
Cost: ★

UTENSILS

1 frying pan
1 saucepan
1 ovenproof dish
1 food processor or blender
1 sieve
OVEN
180°C (350°F/Gas Mark 4)

STALKS AND
·SHOOTS·

·ASPARAGUS·

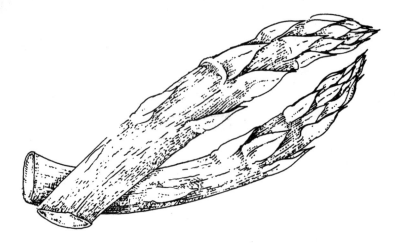

W̶E KNOW THAT asparagus featured in the lives of the Ancient Egyptians, since it is mentioned in their hieroglyphics. The Greeks used it as an aphrodisiac, claiming that it sprang from a ram's horn planted in the earth. The Romans used it when preparing their birds' tongue pâtés, while the Arabs introduced it to the many countries they conquered during their period of expansion, most notably to Spain, where it still flourishes. After a long period of oblivion, asparagus made its reappearance in eighteenth-century Europe, and once more achieved great popularity.

Wild asparagus grows as a weed in the great uncultivated sandy plains of southern central Europe and North Africa. As a cultivated plant, it prefers sandy soil, sheltered from sun, heat and drying winds.

◇ BUYING ASPARAGUS ◇

The stalks should be smooth, without too many opened scales at the tip; they should be crisp and feel damp when snapped. The yellower a stalk becomes, the more it betrays its age and unsuitability for cooking.

For ease of cooking, choose stalks of uniform size; if you buy them in bundles, they have already been graded by the grower. Avoid over-long stalks: the extra weight is not always reflected in the end result.

Asparagus stalks sold as 'green' should in fact show green and white in equal proportions. When served, all of a white variety should be edible, and most of any green stalks.

Asparagus is generally served by itself; when it is served with fish or meat, choose the blander types, so that the highly individual flavour of the asparagus is not blurred. Allow about 450 g (1 lb) untrimmed weight, per person.

Store for as short a time as possible before using, to enjoy maximum flavour. Asparagus seems expensive when compared to most other vegetables, but the individuality and savour of a dish of asparagus is far greater than that of many another first course.

◇ PREPARING ASPARAGUS ◇

Begin by removing any open scales around the tip, then peel the asparagus, using a potato peeler, and cutting away from the tip. The stalks should be peeled as evenly as possible, for attractive presentation and even cooking.

As the stalks are peeled, put them into a pan of cold water. Gather all the prepared stalks into a bundle, and tie firmly but not tightly, using fine string. You may prefer to make as many bundles as you have guests.

◇ COOKING ASPARAGUS ◇

Bring a large saucepan of well-salted water to the boil (an oval pan is the most convenient shape to handle) and gently slide in the bundle(s). They will float; a piece of muslin or a clean tea-towel covering the surface of the water will retain the steam and ensure even cooking. Allow 5–12 minutes, depending upon the size and freshness of the stalks. You may test for doneness by inserting the point of a small, sharp knife where the green and white parts of the stalk merge. Cooked asparagus should not be crunchy, but should retain a slight firmness throughout the stalk.

When the asparagus is cooked, remove the bundle(s) from the pan, taking care not to break off any tips. Plunge the asparagus into iced water for 10 seconds, to prevent further cooking, and drain on a tea-towel.

Asparagus may be served while still warm, or allowed to cool. It may then be reheated (after an interval of a few hours only) in its own cooking water. Do not allow it to boil, if reheated. All types of asparagus may be frozen, but the white varieties are best for this purpose. Asparagus should be packed in foil trays for freezing, and thawed in boiling water.

◇ ASPARAGUS VINAIGRETTE ◇

◇ Prepare and cook the asparagus as described above.
◇ Prepare the vinaigrette by mixing together the oils and vinegar, adding a little more of each, in the correct proportions if necessary, to allow a generous quantity for each person. Season to taste with salt and pepper.
◇ Peel and finely chop the shallot and add. If using the herbs, add them to the dressing at the last minute, so that you can enjoy the freshness of the herb taste without any of the acidity or bitterness that may occur if the herbs soak in the dressing for too long. Serve the vinaigrette in a jug, to accompany the asparagus.

INGREDIENTS

1.8 kg (4 lb) plump asparagus
2.5 ml (½ tsp) hazelnut oil
75 ml (5 tbsp) groundnut (peanut) oil
10 ml (2 tsp) sherry vinegar
30 ml (2 tbsp) wine vinegar
salt and pepper
1 small shallot
chopped parsley or chives (optional)

FIRST COURSE

SERVES 4
Preparation: 10 minutes
Cooking: 10 minutes
Difficulty: *
Cost: **

UTENSILS

1 large saucepan (ideally oval)
1 bowl

41

◇ ASPARAGUS WITH ASPARAGUS HERB CREAM ◇

◇ Prepare and cook the asparagus as described on page 41.
◇ Trim about 3 cm (1¼ inches) from the bottom of the cooked asparagus stalks. Reduce these trimmings to a purée in a food mill or food processor, then sieve to make a smooth purée. Discard the debris.
◇ Put the finely chopped shallot and the wine into a small saucepan. Boil until the liquid has evaporated and the mixture is almost dry. Add the cream and bring to the boil. Reduce to form a smooth sauce: when the surface bubbles, the cream should be sufficiently reduced.
◇ Add the asparagus purée to the pan, mix well and return to the heat for 30 seconds. Then add the chopped herbs. Check the seasoning and serve in a sauceboat, to accompany the asparagus.

INGREDIENTS

1.8 kg (4 lb) plump asparagus
1 shallot, finely chopped
50 ml (2 fl oz/¼ cup) dry white wine
400 ml (14 fl oz/1⅔ cups) double
(heavy) cream
30 ml (2 tbsp) finely chopped tarragon,
chives or parsley

FIRST COURSE

SERVES 4
Preparation: 10–15 minutes
Cooking: 10 minutes
Difficulty: ★★
Cost: ★★

UTENSILS

1 large saucepan (ideally oval)
1 food mill or food processor
1 small saucepan
1 sieve

◇ ASPARAGUS WITH HOLLANDAISE SAUCE AND CHERVIL ◇

◇ Prepare and cook the asparagus as described on page 41.
◇ To make the Hollandaise sauce, clarify the butter by heating it very gently in a small saucepan. When it begins to foam, heat for 1 minute longer. Skim off the foam. A whitish deposit will form at the bottom of the pan. Skim well again. Pour the melted butter gently into another container, leaving the sediment in the pan.
◇ Put the egg yolks into a small saucepan with 30 ml (2 tbsp) cold water. Heat VERY gently – the yolks must not curdle – whisking vigorously to thicken the yolks. As the mixture begins to froth and turn pale, add the butter, a little at a time, whisking constantly. When all the butter has been added, whisk in the lemon juice.
◇ Season to taste with salt and pepper, then stir in the chervil. Serve in a sauceboat, to accompany the warm asparagus.

INGREDIENTS

1.8 kg (4 lb) plump asparagus
100 g (4 oz/1 stick) butter
2 egg yolks
juice of ½ lemon
salt and pepper
15–30 ml (1–2 tbsp) chopped chervil

FIRST COURSE

SERVES 4
Preparation: 10 minutes
Cooking: 10 minutes
Difficulty: ★
Cost: ★★

UTENSILS

1 large saucepan (ideally oval)
1 small saucepan
1 skimming ladle
1 balloon whisk

◇ Prepare and cook the asparagus as described on page 41. If the main cooking is done any length of time before the meal is to be served, keep the water in which the asparagus was cooked; reheat this and plunge the asparagus in it briefly, just before serving, to reheat.

◇ Meanwhile, prepare the mayonnaise. Make sure that the ingredients and utensils are at room temperature, or even slightly above, so that it will emulsify easily. Put the egg yolk and vinegar in a small warm bowl. Whisk vigorously and begin adding the oil in drops, beating constantly. When the sauce starts to thicken, add the oil in a thin stream, but do not add the oil faster than it can be absorbed. Season to taste with salt and pepper. Alternatively make the mayonnaise in a food processor.

◇ Prepare the sauce by whisking the mayonnaise with the cream, vinegars and paprika. The sauce should not be too thick; a little more vinegar may be added, if necessary.

◇ Add the chives to the sauce just before serving. Serve in a sauceboat, to accompany the warm asparagus.

INGREDIENTS

1.8 kg (4 lb) plump asparagus
100 ml (4 fl oz/½ cup) single (light) cream
10 ml (2 tsp) red wine vinegar
5 ml (1 tsp) sherry vinegar
7.5 ml (1½ tsp) paprika
15 ml (1 tbsp) chopped chives
FOR THE MAYONNAISE
1 egg yolk
50 ml (2 fl oz/3½ tbsp) distilled malt vinegar
200 ml (7 fl oz/⅞ cup) groundnut (peanut) oil
salt and pepper

FIRST COURSE

SERVES 4
Preparation: 10 minutes
Cooking: 10 minutes
Difficulty: ★
Cost: ★★

UTENSILS

1 large saucepan (ideally oval)
1 balloon whisk
1 bowl

◇ Prepare and chop all the stock vegetables. Put the chicken bones and giblets, and the prepared vegetables and herbs into a large saucepan. Add the wine and 1.4 litres (2½ pints/1½ quarts) cold water. Bring to the boil, then simmer gently for 40 minutes, skimming frequently. Strain off the liquid and discard the debris.

◇ Prepare and cook the asparagus as described on page 41. While the asparagus is cooking, poach the chicken breasts very gently in the stock for 7–10 minutes. Remove the chicken breasts, cut them into strips and keep warm. Trim 3 cm (1¼ inches) from the bottom of the cooked asparagus stalks. Reduce these trimmings to a purée in a food mill or food processor, then sieve to make a smooth purée. Discard the debris.

◇ Pour 200 ml (7 fl oz/⅞ cup) of the chicken poaching stock into a small saucepan. Boil rapidly to reduce by three-quarters. Add the cream and reduce to make a smooth sauce: when bubbles form on the surface, the sauce should be ready.

◇ Put one-quarter of this sauce into another small saucepan and mix in the asparagus purée. Check the seasoning and bring back to the boil.

◇ Pour a pool of the white cream sauce on to each heated individual serving plate. Arrange the chicken strips and the asparagus on this. Pour a ring of the green sauce round the edge of each plate and serve.

INGREDIENTS

4 chicken breasts, boned
200 ml (7 fl oz/⅞ cup) double (heavy)
cream
16 spears thin green asparagus
FOR THE CHICKEN
STOCK
50 g (2 oz) carrots
50 g (2 oz) onions
50 g (2 oz) mushrooms
1 onion
1 celery stalk
1 leek
450 g (1 lb) chicken bones and giblets
1 garlic clove
1 thyme sprig
1 bay leaf
3 parsley sprigs
100 ml (4 fl oz/½ cup) dry white wine

FIRST COURSE

SERVES 4
Preparation: 30–45 minutes
Cooking: 40–50 minutes
Difficulty: ★★★
Cost: ★★

UTENSILS

2 large saucepans (1 ideally oval)
2 small saucepans
1 sieve
1 skimming ladle
1 food mill or food processor

◇ FILLETS OF SOLE WITH WHITE ASPARAGUS ◇

Towards the end of the season, one may find small, short asparagus which is neither graded nor sold in bundles. It is generally quite cheap and would be especially suitable for this dish.

◇ First make the fish stock: put the sole trimmings into a large bowl and leave in the sink under a gently-running cold tap for 10 minutes, to chill and wash them well. (If this is not done, the stock may taste unpleasantly strong.) Then put the washed trimmings, the parsley or chervil and the roughly chopped ½ onion into a large saucepan with 1 litre (1¾ pints/1 quart) cold water. Bring to the boil, then simmer gently for 10 minutes, skimming frequently. Strain.

◇ Skin and seed the tomato; dice the flesh. Peel and finely chop the shallot. Melt the butter in a small sauté pan and cook the tomato and the shallot very gently for a few minutes, until the tomato is soft and pulpy.

◇ Prepare and cook the asparagus as described on page 41. Cut about 3 cm (1¼ inches) from the bottom of the cooked asparagus stalks. Reduce these trimmings to a purée in a food mill or food processor, then sieve to make a smooth purée. Discard the debris.

◇ Poach the fillets of sole for 1–2 minutes in the fish stock; remove and keep warm.

◇ Bring the stock to a fast boil and boil to reduce for 10 minutes, then add the cream. Continue to reduce, over a slightly lower heat, until the bubbles just reach the surface. Pass the mixture through a sieve. Stir in the asparagus purée. Reheat the puréed tomato.

◇ Arrange 2 sole fillets in a cross shape on each heated individual serving plate. Coat them with the asparagus sauce. Garnish with asparagus and the puréed tomato. Sprinkle with parsley.

INGREDIENTS

1 tomato
½ shallot
100 g (4 oz/1 stick) butter
550 g (1¼ lb) white asparagus
2 soles, each weighing about 800 g
(1¾ lb), each divided into 4 fillets
200 ml (7 fl oz/⅞ cup) double (heavy)
cream
1 bunch of parsley, chopped
FOR THE FISH STOCK
550 g (1¼ lb) sole bones and trimmings
10 ml (2 tsp) chopped parsley, or a few
chervil sprigs
½ onion

MAIN COURSE

SERVES 4
Preparation: 15–30 minutes
Cooking: 15 minutes
Difficulty: ★★★
Cost: ★★★

UTENSILS

3 large saucepans (1 ideally oval)
1 skimming ladle
1 small sauté pan
1 food mill or food processor
1 colander
1 sieve

◇ LOBSTER MEDALLIONS WITH ASPARAGUS MOUSSE ◇

◇ To make the asparagus mousse, cut off the asparagus tips and reserve for use in another dish. Prepare and cook the stalks as described on page 41. Reduce them to a purée in a food mill or food processor, then sieve to make a smooth purée and allow to cool. Discard the debris.

◇ Put 100 ml (4 fl oz/½ cup) of the cream in a saucepan. Bring it to the boil and reduce, until smooth and thick. Add the gelatine and the asparagus purée. Mix well and allow the mixture to cool.

◇ Whip 150 ml (5 fl oz/⅔ cup) of the remaining cream until it forms soft peaks. Using a fork, blend this with the asparagus mixture. Chill in the refrigerator until set.

◇ Clean and chop the onions and carrots. Put them into a large saucepan with 1 litre (1¾ pints/1 quart) cold water, the bouquet garni and the vinegar. Immerse the live lobster in this mixture. Return to the boil, then simmer gently for 15 minutes.

◇ Remove the pan from the heat and leave the lobster to stand in the cooking water for 10 minutes. Then remove it from the pan and allow to cool completely. Reserve the cooking liquid.

◇ Separate the tail section from the body, remove the shell and cut the tail-meat into medallions.

◇ Scrape out all the other edible parts of the lobster from the shell. Add 50 ml (2 fl oz/¼ cup) of the cooking liquid, blend in a food processor or food mill and put through a sieve. Allow to cool, then add the remaining cream and the lemon juice and season to taste with salt and pepper.

◇ To serve, pour a pool of the lobster cream sauce on to each heated individual serving plate. Add 2 or 3 scoops of asparagus mousse (shaped with 2 spoons, or use a small ice-cream scoop) and a few lobster medallions. Sprinkle with parsley or chervil.

INGREDIENTS

450 g (1 lb) asparagus
350 ml (12 fl oz/1½ cups) double (heavy) cream
5 ml (1 tsp) powdered gelatine
100 g (4 oz) onions
50 g (2 oz) carrots
1 bouquet garni
150 ml (5 fl oz/⅔ cup) malt vinegar
1 lobster weighing 800 g (1¾ lb)
juice of 1 lemon
salt and pepper
15 ml (1 tbsp) chopped parsley or chervil

FIRST COURSE

SERVES 4
Preparation: 15–30 minutes
Cooking: 15–30 minutes
Difficulty: ★★★
Cost: ★★★

UTENSILS

2 large saucepans (1 ideally oval)
1 food processor or food mill
1 fine sieve
1 small saucepan
1 balloon whisk

◇ COLD GREEN ASPARAGUS SOUP WITH LANGOUSTINES ◇

◇ Clean and chop all the vegetables except the asparagus. Put them into a large saucepan with 1.7 litres (3 pints/2 quarts) cold water and the herbs. Bring to the boil, then simmer for about 15 minutes. Remove the vegetables and return the pan to the heat. Bring to the boil again and add the langoustines. Return to the boil and cook for about 1 minute, then immediately remove the langoustines and drain them thoroughly.

◇ When the langoustines are cool enough to handle, separate the tail part of each one from the body and claws. Remove the flesh from the tailshell; split each tail open to remove the black threadlike gut. Reserve all the shells and body parts, together with the cooking liquid.

◇ To make the soup, prepare and cook the asparagus as described on page 41. Cut off the tips and reserve for garnishing. Reduce the stalks to a purée in a food mill or food processor, then sieve, to make a smooth purée. Discard the debris.

◇ Crush the langoustine shells and trimmings. Put them into a large sauté pan and pour over the reserved cooking liquid, to cover. Simmer for 20 minutes, then pass through a sieve, pressing well with the back of a spoon. Boil the liquid to reduce to about 450 ml (15 fl oz/2 cups). Allow to cool.

◇ Add the cream and the asparagus purée. Mix well and allow to get completely cold.

◇ Ladle the soup into soup plates and divide the asparagus tips and the langoustine tails equally among them.

INGREDIENTS

50 g (2 oz) carrots
50 g (2 oz) onions
1 small celery stalk
1 small leek
1 thyme sprig
1 bay leaf
1 coriander sprig
24 langoustines (Pacific prawns are also suitable)
450 g (1 lb) thin green asparagus
30 ml (2 tbsp) double (heavy) cream

FIRST COURSE

SERVES 4–6
Preparation: 10 minutes
Cooking: 20 minutes
Difficulty: ★★
Cost: ★★★

UTENSILS

2 large saucepans (1 ideally oval)
1 sieve
1 colander
1 food mill or food processor
1 large sauté pan

◇ BRAISED VEAL WITH ASPARAGUS ◇

◇ Heat the oven to 180°C (350°F/Gas Mark 4). Melt 50 g (2 oz/4 tbsp) of the butter in a flameproof casserole. Brown the veal on all sides. Add the carrots, cut into chunks about 5 cm (2 inches) long, and the roughly chopped onions. Season with salt and pepper. Lower the heat, add a wine glass of water and deglaze the casserole, scraping the base well to loosen any sediment.

◇ Cook the veal in the oven for about 1 hour, until tender, basting regularly. Add a little more water if necessary. When cooked, season again with salt and pepper.

◇ While the veal is cooking, prepare and cook the asparagus as described on page 41. When the veal is ready, fry the cooked asparagus gently in the remaining butter.

◇ Carve the veal and arrange the slices on a heated serving platter. Put the asparagus, onions and carrots around them. Coat with the meat juices from the casserole.

INGREDIENTS

75 g (3 oz/6 tbsp) butter
800 g (1¾ lb) rolled loin of veal
150 g (5 oz) carrots
100 g (4 oz) onions
salt and pepper
450 g (1 lb) asparagus

MAIN COURSE

SERVES 4
Preparation: 15–20 minutes
Cooking: 1 hour
Difficulty: ★★
Cost: ★★

UTENSILS

1 flameproof casserole
1 large saucepan (ideally oval)
1 frying pan
OVEN
180°C (350°F/Gas Mark 4)

◇ WARM OYSTERS WITH ASPARAGUS ◇

◇ Prepare and cook the asparagus as described on page 41.

◇ Trim about 2.5 cm (1 inch) from the bottom of the cooked asparagus stalks. Reduce these trimmings to a purée in a food mill or food processor, then sieve to make a smooth purée. Discard the debris.

◇ Open the oysters. Wrap the hand in which you hold the oyster in a tea-towel, for protection, unless you are skilled in this art. If you do not have an oyster-knife, a round-bladed knife will be more useful than a pointed one. Introduce the blade between the two shells and lever them apart. Save the oyster liquid; if necessary, put it through a fine strainer to remove any pieces of shell.

◇ Put the oyster flesh into a saucepan. Warm through over the lowest possible heat; they should be just tepid, and should not cook.

◇ Put 50 ml (2 fl oz/¼ cup) of the reserved oyster liquid into a small saucepan. Add the butter and season with pepper, but do not add salt. Heat until the mixture just begins to boil, whisking to blend well. Whisk in the asparagus purée.

◇ Pour a pool of this sauce on to each heated individual serving plate. Arrange the oysters and asparagus on top.

INGREDIENTS

24 small green asparagus spears
12 oysters, size 2
100 g (4 oz/1 stick) butter
pepper

FIRST COURSE

SERVES 4
Preparation: 10 minutes
Cooking: 10 minutes
Difficulty: ★★
Cost: ★★★

UTENSILS

1 large saucepan (ideally oval)
1 food mill or food processor
1 balloon whisk

GLOBE
◆ARTICHOKES◆

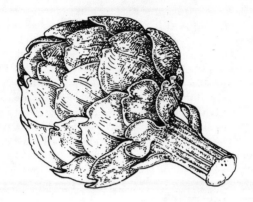

LIKE THE CARDOON, to which it is related, the globe artichoke grows wild in the Mediterranean area where it originated. The Egyptians pickled it in brine, the Greeks mentioned it frequently in their writings and the Romans considered it one of their most extravagant dishes. It was also the Romans who introduced the globe artichoke to the rest of Europe.

In medieval France, the artichoke was a rarity believed to be an aphrodisiac; it returned to fashion at the time of Catherine de Medicis, who ate it garnished with cock'scombs. It was not until after the First World War that the artichoke featured as an everyday vegetable in France. More recently it has become an important part of Brittany's export trade.

Artichokes contain Vitamins A and C, but very little carbohydrate, fat or protein.

◇ BUYING ARTICHOKES ◇
A good artichoke should weigh heavy in the hand and be pure green with no blackish patches on the leaves. These should be crisp, closely packed and scarcely opened; once the leaves begin to open, the artichoke is past its best. The edible parts are the heart and the lower fleshy part of each leaf.

◇ COOKING ARTICHOKES ◇
Bring a large saucepan of water to the boil, adding 7 g ($\frac{1}{4}$ oz/1$\frac{1}{2}$ tsp) salt per litre (1$\frac{3}{4}$ pints/1 quart) water. Add the rinsed artichokes. Cooking time will vary according to the size of the artichoke; 35–45 minutes is usual, but longer may be necessary. The artichoke is cooked when an outside leaf can be removed easily. Drain the artichokes upside down in a colander, if they are to be eaten whole.

It is important to snap the stalk, rather than cut it. In this way it is possible to pull away most of the long fibres which are quite deeply anchored in the heart, and which are too stringy to eat.

Grasp the artichoke firmly and bend the stalk until it snaps. Then pull away the first few outer rows of leaves, by tugging them downwards, until the tender inside leaves are visible. Cut the artichoke in half crossways, about halfway up. With a small stainless steel knife, trim around the base, starting at the stalk. The hairy 'choke' will appear as you remove more of the leaves.

Once cut, artichokes tend to blacken. Avoid this by rubbing the artichoke with the cut side of a half lemon. Then put each prepared artichoke heart into a bowl of cold water with some lemon juice or vinegar. Put 15 ml (1 tbsp) flour into a sieve. Holding the sieve under the tap, fill a large saucepan with cold water. Add salt and the juice of a lemon. Put in the artichoke hearts and cover them with a piece of muslin (cheesecloth) so that they will stay submerged and cook evenly. Bring to the boil and cook for 12–15 minutes.

Artichoke hearts prepared in this way can be kept for 2–3 days if:

a) they are kept in a cool place;
b) they remain in their cooking liquid;
c) the choke is not removed.

◇ ARTICHOKE HEARTS WITH MOUSSERONS ◇

Mousserons are a wild mushroom, a member of the Agaric family. Commercially cultivated mushrooms or oyster mushrooms may be substituted, but the flavour of the dish will be less intense.

◇ Prepare and cook the artichoke hearts as described above, for 10 minutes only in a blanching liquid using the flour, lemon juice and a generous amount of salt; they must remain fairly firm.

◇ Remove the fibrous choke; it may be pulled away with the fingers or scraped away with a teaspoon. Cut each heart into quarters. Sauté them in the butter for about 5 minutes. Then add the mousserons, stalks removed. (If using cultivated mushrooms, wipe the caps and trim away any gritty stalks.) Season with salt and pepper and cook for 2–5 minutes, until the mousserons are tender.

◇ Just before serving sprinkle with the shallot and parsley.

INGREDIENTS

12 artichokes
15 ml (1 tbsp) flour
juice of 1 lemon
25 g (1 oz/2 tbsp) butter
450 g (1 lb) mousserons
½ shallot, peeled and finely chopped
a little finely chopped parsley

FIRST COURSE

SERVES 4
Preparation: 15 minutes
Cooking: 25 minutes
Difficulty: ★
Cost: ★★★

UTENSILS

1 small stainless steel knife
1 large saucepan
1 sauté pan

◇ ARTICHOKES A LA GRECQUE ◇

◇ Prepare the artichoke hearts as described on page 50, remove the chokes and rub with lemon juice. Do not boil the artichoke hearts.

◇ Heat the olive oil in a fairly large sauté pan. Add the artichoke hearts, salt and pepper to taste, the coriander, and bouquet garni. Pour in just enough water to cover. Bring to the boil, then simmer for 15 minutes.

◇ Allow the mixture to cool. Then remove the bouquet garni and add the tomato, skinned, seeded and cut into small dice.

INGREDIENTS

12–16 small artichokes
juice of 1 lemon
50 ml (2 fl oz/¼ cup) olive oil
salt and coarsely ground black pepper
5–10 ml (1–2 tsp) coriander seeds
1 bouquet garni
1 tomato

MAIN COURSE OR SIDE DISH

SERVES 4
Preparation: 15 minutes
Cooking: 15 minutes
Difficulty: ★
Cost: ★★

UTENSILS

1 small stainless steel knife
1 sauté pan

◇ SALAD OF ARTICHOKES WITH HORSERADISH ◇

◇ Prepare and cook the artichoke hearts in a blanching liquid using the lemon juice, flour and salt as described on page 50.

◇ Remove the chokes from the artichoke hearts. Cut the hearts into 5 mm (¼ inch) cubes. Leave them to get cold.

◇ Put the cream into a salad bowl. Add salt and a very little pepper. Sprinkle in a small quantity of grated horseradish, to taste. Mix well.

◇ Add the cubed artichoke hearts. Turn them in the cream sauce so that they are well coated. Sprinkle with a few chopped chives.

INGREDIENTS

12–16 artichokes
juice of 1 lemon
15 ml (1 tbsp) flour
salt
100 ml (4 fl oz/½ cup) double (heavy) cream
pepper
a little freshly grated horseradish
chopped chives

FIRST COURSE

SERVES 4
Preparation: 15 minutes
Cooking: 20 minutes
Difficulty: ★★
Cost: ★★

UTENSILS

1 small stainless steel knife
1 large saucepan
1 salad bowl
1 grater

◇ FRICASSEE OF BABY SQUID AND ARTICHOKES ◇

◇ Prepare and cook the artichoke hearts as described on page 50, using half the lemon juice for the blanching liquid with the flour and salt. When the liquid comes to the boil, cook the artichokes for 8–10 minutes.

◇ Meanwhile, clean the squid and cut them into strips 5 mm ($\frac{1}{4}$ inch) wide. For this recipe, you may also use the heads and tentacles of the squid, and these do not need to be cut up.

◇ Remove the chokes from the cooked artichoke hearts. Cut the hearts into quarters. Fry them in the butter, in a large sauté pan, for 2–3 minutes. Remove them from the pan and keep warm.

◇ Put the squid into the same pan and turn up the heat so that they begin to colour. Cook them for only 1–2 minutes; any longer and they will become rubbery.

◇ Return the artichoke hearts to the pan for a minute or so. Add salt, pepper and lemon juice in generous quantities. Tip the mixture into a serving dish and sprinkle with chopped parsley.

INGREDIENTS

12–16 artichokes

juice of 2 lemons

15 ml (1 tbsp) flour

salt

550 g (1¼ lb) baby squid

75 g (3 oz/6 tbsp) butter

pepper

1 small bunch of parsley, chopped

FIRST OR MAIN COURSE

SERVES 4

Preparation: 15 minutes

Cooking: 15 minutes

Difficulty: ★

Cost: ★★

UTENSILS

1 small stainless steel knife

1 large saucepan

1 large sauté pan

◇ SALAD OF ARTICHOKE HEARTS AND ANCHOVIES ◇

◇ Prepare and cook the artichoke hearts as described on page 50, using the flour, salt and all but 15 ml (1 tbsp) of the lemon juice for the blanching liquid. Remove the choke from each artichoke. Cut the hearts into strips about 2.5 cm (1 inch) wide. Arrange the strips attractively on individual serving plates.

◇ Reduce 8 of the anchovies to a purée in a blender or food processor. Add this purée to a dressing made from the olive oil, the remaining lemon juice and pepper to taste. Taste before adding any salt; you may need none at all.

◇ Spoon the dressing over the artichoke heart strips. Decorate with the remaining anchovy fillets, cut in half lengthways.

INGREDIENTS

12 artichokes

15 ml (1 tbsp) flour

salt

juice of 1 lemon

12 anchovy fillets, soaked in milk if very salty

45 ml (3 tbsp) olive oil

pepper

FIRST COURSE

SERVES 4

Preparation: 15 minutes

Cooking time: 20 minutes

Difficulty: ★

Cost: ★

UTENSILS

1 small stainless steel knife

1 large saucepan

1 blender or food processor

◇ Prepare and cook the artichoke hearts in a blanching liquid using the flour, lemon juice and salt as described on page 50. Remove the chokes. Reduce the artichoke hearts to a purée in a food processor or food mill.

◇ Heat the oven to 170°C (325°F/Gas Mark 3).

◇ Mix the egg yolks with the cream and season with salt and pepper. Add the artichoke purée and mix well.

◇ Grease 8 ramekins with some of the butter. Put a layer of the artichoke cream, 1 cm (½ inch) deep, inside each ramekin. Scatter the truffle trimmings on top. Divide the remaining artichoke cream among the ramekins.

◇ Put the ramekins into a large ovenproof dish or roasting pan. Pour in boiling water to come halfway up the sides of the ramekins. Cover and cook in the oven for 20–30 minutes, until set.

◇ To turn out the custards, tap all round the edge of each ramekin, while holding it at an angle. Turn each custard out on to a plate.

◇ Coat each custard with a sauce made from the juice from the truffle tin or jar, reheated with the remaining butter. Season lightly with salt and pepper before serving.

INGREDIENTS

6 artichokes

15 ml (1 tbsp) flour

juice of 1 lemon

salt

3 egg yolks

200 ml (7 fl oz/⅞ cup) double (heavy) cream

pepper

25 g (1 oz/2 tbsp) butter

25 g (1 oz) truffle trimmings

FIRST COURSE OR SIDE DISH

SERVES 4–8

Preparation: 15 minutes

Cooking: about 1 hour

Difficulty: ★★

Cost: ★★★

UTENSILS

1 small stainless steel knife

1 large saucepan

1 food processor or foodmill

8 ramekins

1 shallow ovenproof dish or roasting pan

OVEN

170°C (325°F/Gas Mark 3)

◇ Put the venison joint into a large bowl. Add the marinade ingredients: sprinkle the venison with the peppercorns, thyme, bay leaf and juniper berries and pour over the olive oil, taking care to cover all the surfaces of the meat. Cover and leave to marinate for 5 days in a cool place, turning the venison each day.

◇ When ready to cook, season the venison with salt and put it into a roasting pan with the butter. Heat the oven to 220°C (425°F/Gas Mark 7). Put in the venison and when the outside is well browned reduce the oven to 180°C (350°F/Gas Mark 4).

◇ Meanwhile, trim and prepare the artichoke hearts as described on page 50 and rub with lemon juice, but do not boil them. Remove the chokes.

◇ When the venison has been cooking for 10 minutes, drain the artichoke hearts well and put them in the roasting pan around the joint. Baste them well with the meat juices.

◇ When the venison is cooked to your liking (about 30 minutes), reduce the oven to the lowest temperature. Wrap the venison in kitchen foil and allow it to rest for 20 minutes. Keep the artichoke hearts warm.

◇ Carve the venison into slices as you would a leg of lamb and arrange the slices with the artichoke hearts on a warmed serving dish. Keep warm while you make the juice.

◇ Drain the juices from the roasting pan into a bowl. Put the pan over a moderate heat and deglaze with the two vinegars, scraping the base and sides well with a wooden spatula in order to loosen any sediment. Allow this mixture to simmer for 5 minutes, then add the reserved meat juices. Mix well. Season to taste with salt and pepper. Serve in a separate sauceboat.

INGREDIENTS

1 haunch of venison, weighing 1.8 kg (4 lb)

salt

75 g (3 oz/6 tbsp) butter

16 artichokes

juice of 1 lemon

50 ml (2 fl oz/¼ cup) sherry vinegar

50 ml (2 fl oz/¼ cup) red wine vinegar

pepper

FOR THE MARINADE

a few crushed black peppercorns

1 thyme sprig

1 bay leaf

a few juniper berries

50 ml (2 fl oz/¼ cup) olive oil

MAIN COURSE

SERVES 6–8

Preparation: 20 minutes

Cooking and resting: 1½ hours

Difficulty: ★★

Cost: ★★★★

UTENSILS

1 large bowl for marinating

1 small stainless steel knife

1 large saucepan

1 roasting pan

kitchen foil

1 wooden spatula

OVEN

220°C (425°F/Gas Mark 7)

◇ Prepare and cook the artichoke hearts in a blanching liquid using the flour, lemon juice and salt as described on page 50. Remove the chokes. Cut the hearts into strips 5 mm (¼ inch) wide and keep warm.

◇ While the artichoke hearts are cooking, begin to prepare the watercress sauce. Put the cream into a small saucepan. Bring it to the boil. Allow it to reduce and thicken.

◇ Wash the watercress and trim away the lower parts of the stalks. Bring a large saucepan of salted water to the boil. Blanch the watercress in the boiling water for 2 minutes, then plunge it into iced water, to prevent further cooking. Drain the watercress well and reduce it to a purée in a blender or food processor.

◇ Melt the butter in a sauté pan. When it is just beginning to brown, add the watercress purée. Season to taste with salt and pepper. Stir for a few seconds. Add the cream. Mix well and check the seasoning.

◇ Spoon a pool of sauce on to each heated individual serving plate and arrange some artichoke strips on top. Serve immediately.

INGREDIENTS

12–16 artichokes
15 ml (1 tbsp) flour
juice of 1 lemon
salt
100 ml (4 fl oz/½ cup) double (heavy) cream
2 bunches of watercress
15 g (½ oz/1 tbsp) butter
pepper

FIRST COURSE

SERVES 4
Preparation: 20 minutes
Cooking: 30 minutes
Difficulty: ★★
Cost: ★★

UTENSILS

1 small stainless steel knife
1 large saucepan
1 small saucepan
1 blender or food processor
1 sauté pan

◆·CARDOONS·◆

THE CARDOON (sometimes called cardoni), a plant which is related to the thistle and the globe artichoke, originated in the Mediterranean islands of Sicily, Sardinia and the Balearics, where it grew wild in hedgerows.

The cardoon is a plant which cannot withstand frost, and will only grow in temperate climates. It is prickly to the touch, though plant research has, over the years, improved and refined the cardoon, so that the varieties most commonly cultivated now are no longer aggressively prickly.

The edible part of the plant is the broad whitish stalks which grow out from a central stalk which may attain a height of 2 m (6 ft). The cardoon is much appreciated in several European countries, and is grown commercially mainly in France and Italy. Although not easily available in Britain, it is well worth trying if you can get it. The flavour is similar to globe artichokes. In Australia it is a weed as widespread and as unpopular as the dandelion in this country. The cardoon has little nutritional value, though it does provide fibre.

◇ BUYING CARDOONS ◇
Avoid blotched or split stalks. Allow 450 g (1 lb) per person.

◇ PREPARING CARDOONS ◇
The white part of the inside leaves is used in cooking. Remove and discard the outer stalks which are generally tough and hollow. Cut the other stalks away from the base. Check that none are hollow at the base. In general, the closer the stalks are to the centre, the less likely it is that there will be any waste. With a small knife peel each stalk, removing the outer skin and any strings. Cut the stalks into pieces about 4 cm (1½ inches) long. Once peeled, cardoon stalks discolour very quickly. Avoid this by placing in a bowl of acidulated water as they are prepared.

◇ COOKING CARDOONS ◇

Prepare a blanching liquid by diluting 25 g (1 oz/3 tbsp) flour in 2 litres (3½ pints/2 quarts) cold water. Add 15 ml (1 tbsp) salt and the juice of ½ lemon. Bring to the boil, stirring constantly. Then add a bouquet garni and the cardoons. Return to the boil and simmer for about 1¼ hours.

The cardoon should feel soft to the touch when cooked.

◇ CHEF'S TIPS ◇

Since cardoon discolours so quickly, it must be cooked as soon as it is prepared.

If the cardoon is not to be used immediately after the preliminary cooking, it should be left in its cooking water. Cover the surface of the water with foil or greased paper so that the vegetable does not come into contact with the air.

◇ ROAST BEEF WITH CARDOONS AND MARROW ◇

◇ Put the marrow-bone into a bowl and leave under a gently running cold tap for about 1 hour.

◇ Meanwhile, prepare the cardoons and cook in a blanching liquid made with the flour, salt, lemon juice and bouquet garni, as described on pages 56–7. Simmer the cardoons for 45–60 minutes, until tender.

◇ While the cardoons are cooking, heat the oven to 180°C (350°F/Gas Mark 4). Melt half the butter in a frying pan and seal the beef on all sides.

◇ Clean and chop the carrot and onion. Put the vegetables and the beef bones into a roasting pan. Set the beef on top of them. Cook in the oven for 5 minutes, then add 100 ml (4 fl oz/½ cup) hot water to the pan. Continue to cook the beef until done to your liking: a rare joint will take about 25 minutes. If the beef is ready before the cardoons, keep it warm.

◇ Cut the bone-marrow into slices about 5 mm (¼ inch) thick. Bring a small saucepan of salted water to the boil and poach the slices for about 2 minutes.

◇ Melt the remaining butter in a sauté pan. Fry the cardoons gently for 1 minute, then add half the cooking juices from the roasting pan. Simmer gently for 2–3 minutes.

◇ Tip the cardoons into a heated serving dish. Arrange the slices of bone-marrow on top; give each slice a grinding of pepper. Carve the beef and arrange the slices on a heated serving platter, with the remainder of the cooking juices poured over.

INGREDIENTS

1 good-sized marrow-bone
1.4 kg (3 lb) cardoons
25 g (1 oz/3 tbsp) flour
15 ml (1 tbsp) salt
juice of ½ lemon
1 bouquet garni
40 g (1½ oz/3 tbsp) butter
½ carrot
½ onion
100 g (4 oz) beef bones
1 boned and rolled beef roast, weighing 800 g (1¾ lb)
pepper

MAIN COURSE

SERVES 4–6
Preparation: 15 minutes
Cooking: 1 hour
Difficulty: ★★
Cost: ★★

UTENSILS

1 medium frying pan
1 large saucepan
1 roasting pan
1 small saucepan
1 sauté pan
1 serving platter
OVEN
180°C (350°F/Gas Mark 4)

◇ POACHED CHICKEN WITH A GRATIN OF CARDOONS ◇

◇ Clean and chop the stock vegetables. Push the clove into one of the onions. Put the chicken carcass or giblets into a large saucepan with the vegetables, peppercorns and bouquet garni. Add 2 litres (3½ pints/2 quarts) cold water. Bring to the boil, then simmer for 20 minutes, skimming regularly. Strain the stock.

◇ Truss the chicken so that it will keep its shape. It should not have any giblets left inside it. Bring the stock to the boil in a large saucepan. Add the chicken, salt and pepper. Simmer for 1½ hours.

◇ Prepare the cardoons as described on page 56. Cook the cardoons in a blanching liquid made with vinegar instead of lemon juice, using half the flour. Add the salt and bouquet garni and simmer for 45 minutes until still slightly firm. Drain well.

◇ Put 250 ml (9 fl oz/1⅛ cups) of the chicken stock into a small saucepan and boil to reduce by half.

◇ In another small saucepan, make a white roux with the butter and the remaining flour. Add the reduced chicken stock and the cream. Stir well and cook gently for 5 minutes. Season to taste with salt and pepper.

◇ Heat the oven to 200°C (400°F/Gas Mark 6).

◇ Butter a gratin dish. Arrange the cardoons in it and pour the sauce over them. Bake in the oven for 15 minutes.

◇ Carve the chicken and arrange the pieces on a heated serving platter. Serve accompanied by the cardoons.

INGREDIENTS

1 chicken weighing 1.6 kg (3½ lb)
1.1 kg (2½ lb) cardoons
30 ml (2 tbsp) vinegar
60 g (2 oz/6 tbsp) flour
15 ml (1 tbsp) salt
1 bouquet garni
50 g (2 oz/4 tbsp) butter
300ml (10 fl oz/1¼ cups) double (heavy) cream
pepper

FOR THE CHICKEN STOCK
2 onions
1 celery stalk
1 leek
1 clove
1 chicken carcass or chicken giblets
a few crushed peppercorns
1 bouquet garni

MAIN COURSE

SERVES 4
Preparation: 15 minutes
Cooking: 1½ hours
Difficulty: ★★
Cost: ★

UTENSILS

2 large saucepans
1 small saucepan
1 gratin dish
1 serving platter
OVEN
200°C (400°F/Gas Mark 6)

◇ Line a 23 cm (9 inch) flat tin with the pastry and bake blind.

◇ Prepare the cardoons as described on page 56. Cook them in a blanching liquid made with the flour, salt, lemon juice and bouquet garni for 45–50 minutes. Drain the cardoons when ready to use.

◇ Cut a small cross in the base of each chestnut. Heat the oil in a large frying pan and add the chestnuts. Their skins will split open. Drain the chestnuts and allow them to cool. Peel them, removing both shell and brown inner skin.

◇ Bring a saucepan of water to the boil. Add the cleaned celery and the chestnuts. Cover and boil for 10 minutes. Drain the chestnuts and break them into small pieces.

◇ Heat the oven to 200°C (400°F/Gas Mark 6).

◇ In a small bowl, mix the cream and egg yolk. Season with salt and pepper. Fry the drained cardoons in the butter. Arrange them in the base of the flan case and sprinkle the chestnut pieces on top. Pour over the cream and egg mixture. Bake in the oven for 15 minutes.

INGREDIENTS

200 g (7 oz) shortcrust pastry
800 g (1¾ lb) cardoons
25 g (1 oz/3 tbsp) flour
15 ml (1 tbsp) salt
juice of ½ lemon
1 bouquet garni
200 g (7 oz) unpeeled chestnuts
100 ml (4 fl oz/½ cup) groundnut (peanut) oil
1 celery stalk
100 ml (4 fl oz/½ cup) double (heavy) cream
1 egg yolk
pepper
25 g (1 oz/2 tbsp) butter

FIRST COURSE

SERVES 4–6
Preparation: 20 minutes
Cooking: 30 minutes
Difficulty: ★
Cost: ★★

UTENSILS

1 large saucepan
1 × 23 cm (9 inch) flan tin (tart pan or pie plate)
1 large frying pan
1 saucepan
1 bowl
OVEN
200°C (400°F/Gas Mark 6)

◆ F E N N E L ◆

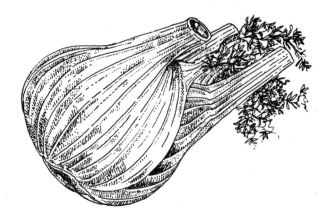

FENNEL ORIGINATED IN southern Europe, and the Egyptians, Greeks and
Romans all used it for medicinal purposes. It was not until the Middle
Ages that the Italians, driven by famine, first used fennel as a foodstuff. The
inhabitants of Nice, much influenced by Italian cuisine, were the first in France
to adopt fennel. It has been known in Britain for some time but has only
recently begun to be in common use.

It is said that an extraction of fennel seed, applied externally, is an excellent
remedy for irritations of the eyes and eyelids, and for migraines. As an
infusion, it is a diuretic, recommended for conditions of the bladder, kidneys
and bile duct.

◇ BUYING FENNEL ◇
Look for pale, firm bulbs with crisp, closely packed leaves. The leaves should
not be green. Avoid blemished or damaged bulbs. Smaller bulbs cook more
quickly and generally give a better appearance to the finished dish.

Allow $\frac{1}{2}$ bulb per person in a side dish.

◇ PREPARING FENNEL ◇
Remove any outer leaves which seem loose, and trim the tops of the stalks if
they seem tough. Hollow out the base of the bulb slightly, as for chicory.
Wash well.

◇ COOKING AND SERVING FENNEL ◇

Fennel may be cooked by several methods.

The whole bulbs may be boiled in salted water for about 15 minutes, then served with butter or a sauce.

They may be blanched for a few minutes in boiling water, then braised in butter, or on a base of onions and carrots, with the addition of a bouquet garni and some meat juices, where possible.

The raw bulbs may also be sliced and sautéed in olive oil for 5–7 minutes.

Fennel is excellent with fish, especially the oilier varieties. It also combines well with other Mediterranean vegetables, such as tomatoes and courgettes (zucchini).

◇ GRATIN OF FENNEL WITH FRESH TOMATO SAUCE ◇

◇ Bring a large saucepan of salted water to the boil. Blanch the fennel for 10 minutes (halve the bulbs before blanching, if they are large).

◇ Heat the oven to 150°C (300°F/Gas Mark 3).

◇ Skin and seed the tomato; cut the flesh into small dice. Peel and finely chop the shallot and garlic. Put the shallot into a sauté pan with the butter and cook gently until transparent. Add the tomato, garlic, olive oil, vegetable stock and the drained fennel. Season with salt and pepper.

◇ Put the mixture into a gratin dish and bake in the oven for 30 minutes, basting with the sauce from time to time. When the fennel is tender, sprinkle with breadcrumbs and brown under a hot grill before serving.

INGREDIENTS

4 fennel bulbs
1 tomato
1 shallot
1 garlic clove
15 g ($\frac{1}{2}$oz/1 tbsp) butter
10 ml (2 tsp) olive oil
50 ml (2 fl oz/$\frac{1}{4}$cup) vegetable stock
salt and pepper
dried breadcrumbs

FIRST COURSE OR SIDE DISH

SERVES 4
Preparation: 5–10 minutes
Cooking: 45 minutes
Difficulty: *
Cost: *

UTENSILS

1 large saucepan
1 sauté pan
1 gratin dish
OVEN
150°C (300°F/Gas Mark 3)

◇ COLD FENNEL RATATOUILLE ◇

Serve well-chilled as an accompaniment to cold meats or fish.

◇ Wash the fennel and cut it into strips.
◇ Skin and seed the tomatoes, cut the flesh into small dice.
◇ Fry the fennel strips in a little olive oil in a sauté pan with a lid until tender (about 5 minutes).
◇ Add the diced tomato and season with salt and pepper. Cover the pan and cook over a moderate heat for 5 minutes.
◇ Remove the pan from the heat, sprinkle the basil over the fennel mixture (if the leaves are large, tear, rather than cut them). Allow the mixture to cool and then chill in the refrigerator.

INGREDIENTS

4 fennel bulbs
3 ripe tomatoes
olive oil
1 small bunch of basil

SIDE DISH

SERVES 4
Preparation: 5 minutes
Cooking: 10 minutes
Difficulty: *
Cost: *

UTENSILS

1 sauté pan with a lid

◇ WARM SALAD OF FENNEL AND LANGOUSTINES ◇

◇ Skin and seed the tomato, cut the flesh into small dice.
◇ Make a vinaigrette by mixing together all the ingredients. Add the diced tomato and set aside.
◇ Wash the fennel and cut it into strips 1 cm (½ inch) wide. Heat 30 ml (2 tbsp) of the olive oil in a sauté pan, add the fennel, cover and cook gently over a low heat for 5–7 minutes. Drain on kitchen paper.
◇ Meanwhile, shell the langoustines and brush the tails with the remaining oil. Cook under a very hot grill for a minute or two on each side, until cooked through.
◇ Arrange a few fennel strips trellis-fashion on each individual serving plate. Add 2–3 langoustine tails to each plate. Coat with the vinaigrette and sprinkle with chopped tarragon.

INGREDIENTS

1 tomato
4 large or 8 small fennel bulbs
45 ml (3 tbsp) olive oil
8–12 langoustines or Pacific prawns
chopped fresh tarragon
FOR THE VINAIGRETTE
30 ml (2 tbsp) olive oil
juice of 1 lemon
10 ml (2 tsp) sherry vinegar
5 ml (1 tsp) coriander seeds

FIRST COURSE

SERVES 4
Preparation: 10 minutes
Cooking: 10 minutes
Difficulty: *
Cost: **

UTENSILS

1 small bowl
1 small sharp knife
1 small saucepan
1 sauté pan
kitchen paper

◇ QUICK-FRIED FENNEL ◇

A simple and quickly prepared dish, reminiscent of the Chinese way of preparing vegetables.

◇ Scrape the carrots and cut them into matchsticks 1 mm ($\frac{1}{16}$ inch) thick and 4 cm ($1\frac{1}{2}$ inches) long.
◇ Peel and slice the shallots thinly. Slice the fennel into strips 1 cm ($\frac{1}{2}$ inch) wide. Cut the courgettes into rounds 2 mm ($\frac{1}{8}$ inch) thick.
◇ Pour enough olive oil into a sauté pan or wok to just cover the base. Add the shallots and carrots. Cook over a high heat, stirring, for 2 minutes. Add the fennel and $\frac{1}{2}$ a wineglass of water. Season with salt and pepper. Cook for a further 4–5 minutes, stirring. Add the courgettes and cook, stirring, for a further 2 minutes.
◇ Check the seasoning, sprinkle with the basil and serve immediately.

INGREDIENTS

2 small carrots
2 shallots
4 fennel bulbs
2 small courgettes (zucchinis)
about 30 ml (2 tbsp) olive oil
salt and pepper
1 small bunch of basil

SIDE DISH

SERVES 4
Preparation: 10–15 minutes
Cooking: 10 minutes
Difficulty: ★
Cost: ★

UTENSILS

1 large sauté pan or wok

◇ SAUTEED CHICKEN WITH FENNEL ◇

◇ Blanch the fennel for 3 minutes in boiling water. Remove and drain well, then cut into quarters.
◇ Heat the olive oil in a large sauté pan and fry the chicken and garlic for 10 minutes, until well-coloured. Add the fennel and cook for a further 10 minutes, until cooked through.
◇ Meanwhile skin and seed the tomato; dice the flesh. Add the tomato to the mixture in the pan 5 minutes before the end of cooking time.
◇ Arrange the chicken and fennel on a heated serving dish, sprinkle with chopped parsley and serve immediately.

INGREDIENTS

4 fennel bulbs
30 ml (2 tbsp) olive oil
1 chicken, cut into 8 pieces
3 garlic cloves (unpeeled)
1 tomato
chopped parsley

MAIN COURSE

SERVES 4
Preparation: 5–10 minutes
Cooking: 25 minutes
Difficulty: ★
Cost: ★

UTENSILS

1 large saucepan
1 large sauté pan
1 small sharp knife
1 small saucepan

63

◇ *FENNEL STUFFED WITH AUBERGINE (EGGPLANT) CAVIAR* ◇

Serve as a cocktail snack, as a first course or as part of a buffet meal.

◇ Wash the fennel. Blanch in boiling water for 3–5 minutes (the fennel should remain firm).
◇ Remove the fennel and drain well. Cut the bulbs into half lengthways and remove the heart from each, to make a small 'boat'.
◇ Prepare the aubergine caviar as described on page 13. The aubergine should be puréed, rather than chopped. Chop the fennel hearts and add to the mixture.
◇ Stuff the fennel boats with the mixture and chill well before serving.

INGREDIENTS

4 small fennel bulbs

FOR THE AUBERGINE
(EGGPLANT) CAVIAR

2 aubergines
200 ml (7 fl oz/⅞ cup) olive oil
2 small shallots
2 ripe tomatoes
200 ml (7 fl oz/⅞ cup) double (heavy) cream
salt and pepper

FIRST COURSE

SERVES 4
Preparation: 25 minutes
Cooking: 20 minutes
Difficulty: ★★
Cost: ★

UTENSILS

1 large saucepan
1 baking tray
1 small sharp knife
1 small saucepan
1 blender or food processor
OVEN
200°C (400°F/Gas Mark 6)

◆·C E L E R Y·◆

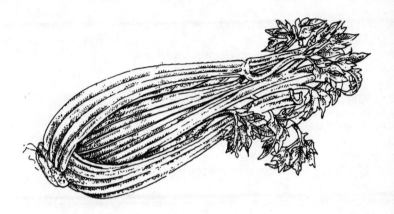

IN ANCIENT GREECE, the athlete's bronze medal was made of celery leaves, and the use of celery leaves as decorative foliage continued until the sixteenth century. Dentists would also apply a celery leaf to any tooth which was to be drawn. Our ancestors also used essence of celery for bone diseases, and prized the plant for its aphrodisiac qualities. Celery contains Vitamin C, with valuable amounts of potassium and calcium.

◇ PREPARING CELERY ◇
Cut the stalks away from the base. Remove any strings, working from top to bottom of the stalk. Wash the stalks well in cold water. Cut larger stalks in 5 cm (2 inch) lengths.

◇ BUYING CELERY ◇
Choose short stalks, 20–25 cm (8–10 inches) long. The best stalks, pale creamy-white, are firm, straight and fleshy. When snapped, a fresh stalk will 'bleed' slightly.

◇ COOKING AND SERVING CELERY ◇
Celery stalks are used in most dishes. For soups and stocks, the leaves may be included.

Celery may be eaten by itself, or raw in mixed salads, or cooked (generally braised). Braised Celery (page 67) is especially good with game and veal. As a salad ingredient, celery goes well with veal, pork and cold fish.

Celery is also used in many basic culinary preparations such as stocks and bouillons. But since celery is quite strongly flavoured, be wary of adding too much.

◇ CHEF'S TIP ◇
When boiling chestnuts, add a stalk of celery to the water; it will bring out their flavour (see Cardoon and Chestnut Tart, page 59).

◇ GRATIN OF CELERY ◇

Use only tender white inner stalks of celery for this recipe.

◇ Wash the celery well, remove any strings and cut into 5 cm (2 inch) lengths.
◇ Blanch the celery for 8 minutes in lightly salted water, then drain well.
◇ Meanwhile, put the cream into a small saucepan. Set it over a low heat and allow to reduce, stirring from time to time. Heat the oven to 200°C (400°F/Gas Mark 6).
◇ Arrange the celery in a buttered ovenproof dish. Pour the reduced cream over it and sprinkle generously with grated cheese.
◇ Bake in the oven for 12–15 minutes. Brown under a hot grill just before serving, if necessary.

INGREDIENTS

450–550 g (1–1¼ lb) celery stalks
salt
400 ml (14 fl oz/1¾ cups) double (heavy) cream
50 g (2 oz) Gruyère cheese, grated
pepper

FIRST COURSE OR SIDE DISH

SERVES 4
Preparation: 10 minutes
Cooking: 15–20 minutes
Difficulty: ★
Cost: ★

UTENSILS

1 large saucepan
1 small saucepan
1 ovenproof dish
OVEN
200°C (400°F/Gas Mark 6)

◇ CELERY SALAD WITH LEMON CREAM DRESSING ◇

This salad is excellent served with cold roast veal or pork, or with fish, in particular salmon. Use only tender white inner stalks of celery for this recipe.

◇ Wash and trim the celery. Slice very thinly.
◇ In a bowl, prepare the lemon cream dressing: mix the cream with the lemon juice and salt and pepper to taste.
◇ Put the celery into a salad bowl. Add the cream mixture. Toss and mix well.

INGREDIENTS

2–3 celery stalks
100 ml (4 fl oz/½ cup) double (heavy) cream
juice of 1 lemon
salt and pepper

SIDE DISH

SERVES 4
Preparation: 5 minutes
Difficulty: ★
Cost: ★

UTENSILS

1 small bowl
1 salad bowl

◇ BRAISED CELERY ◇

Delicious when served with roast game or stewed veal.

◇ Prepare and trim the celery, discarding the tough outer stalks. Cut them into 5 cm (2 inch) lengths. Wash well. Blanch the celery for 5 minutes in boiling water, then drain.
◇ Scrape and wash the carrots. Cut them into rounds. Peel and thinly slice the onions. Heat the oven to 180°C (350°F/Gas Mark 4).
◇ Heat a little oil in a flameproof casserole. Fry the onion and carrot gently until the onion is transparent.
◇ Arrange the celery on top of this mixture. Add salt, pepper and the bouquet garni. Cover with the stock, or with the water and butter.
◇ Cover and braise in the oven for 30–45 minutes, until the celery is tender.

INGREDIENTS

450–550 g (1¼ lb) celery (2 heads)
2 carrots
2 onions
groundnut (peanut) or olive oil
salt and pepper
1 bouquet garni
450 ml (15 fl oz/1¾ cups) veal stock or
50 g (2 oz/4 tbsp) butter and 450 ml
(15 fl oz/1¾ cups) water

SIDE DISH

SERVES 4
Preparation: 10 minutes
Cooking: 30–45 minutes
Difficulty: ★
Cost: ★

UTENSILS

1 flameproof casserole
1 large saucepan
OVEN
180°C (350°F/Gas Mark 4)

◇ CELERY CANAPES ◇

Use only tender white inner stalks of celery for this recipe.

◇ Cut the celery into 5 cm (2 inch) lengths. Wash, drain and dry thoroughly in a tea-towel.
◇ In a bowl, mash together the butter and Roquefort, to make a smooth paste. Add a generous quantity of pepper. Stuff the celery pieces with this mixture.

INGREDIENTS

150–200 g (5–7 oz) celery stalks
(about 3)
25 g (1 oz/2 tbsp) butter
50 g (2 oz) Roquefort cheese
pepper

COCKTAIL SNACK

SERVES 4–6
Preparation: 10 minutes
Difficulty: ★
Cost: ★

UTENSILS

1 bowl
1 spatula

◆ R H U B A R B ◆

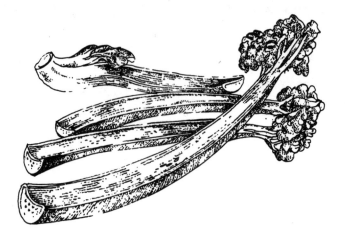

R HUBARB ORIGINATED IN China and Tibet and was originally used as a medicinal plant, since it is an excellent laxative and provides plenty of potassium and calcium with some Vitamin A and C. With its high oxalic acid content it should be avoided by those who suffer from kidney stones. When Magellan brought rhubarb to Europe, it continued to be regarded as a medicament until the English began to cook with it in the eighteenth century.

◇ BUYING RHUBARB ◇
Look for fleshy stalks which may be green or pink.

◇ PREPARING RHUBARB ◇
Trim the stalks, removing all the leaves, which contain enough oxalic acid to be harmful, and must not be eaten.

◇ CHEF'S TIP ◇
Rhubarb freezes perfectly and there is no need to blanch it. Wash, dry well and pack into plastic bags.

◇ CALF'S LIVER WITH RHUBARB ◇

◇ Peel the rhubarb and cut it into 3 cm (1¼ inch) lengths. Slice lengthways into sticks 1 cm (½ inch) wide and 2 mm (⅛ inch) thick.

◇ Put the rhubarb into a bowl, sprinkle generously with sea salt, leave to degorge for about 10 minutes and drain well, then blanch in boiling water for 2–3 minutes and drain well.

◇ Melt about 25 g (1 oz/2 tbsp) of the butter in a frying pan, add the rhubarb and sugar and fry gently until the rhubarb colours slightly and the juices begin to caramelize.

◇ Meanwhile, fry the liver in the remaining butter in another frying pan, allowing it to remain pink in the middle as this way it will be more tender than if cooked all the way through.

◇ Arrange the liver and rhubarb on a heated serving dish and keep warm. Deglaze the liver pan with the vinegars, scraping the base of the pan well with a wooden spatula, and allow to reduce.

◇ Coat the liver with the pan juices, garnish with parsley and serve immediately.

INGREDIENTS

450 g (1 lb) rhubarb
100 g (4 oz/1 stick) butter
a pinch of sugar
4 slices calf's liver
20 ml (4 tsp) sherry vinegar
20 ml (4 tsp) red wine vinegar
parsley sprigs

MAIN COURSE

SERVES 4
Preparation: 20 minutes
Cooking: 5–10 minutes
Difficulty: *
Cost: *

UTENSILS

1 bowl
1 saucepan
2 frying pans

◇ SWEETBREADS WITH RHUBARB ◇

◇ Peel the rhubarb, cut into 3 cm (1¼ inch) lengths, then into strips about 1 cm (½ inch) wide and 2 mm (⅛ inch) thick. Put the rhubarb into a bowl with a handful of sea salt and leave to degorge for about 10 minutes, then rinse, drain and blanch for 2–3 minutes in boiling water. Run cold water over the rhubarb to prevent further cooking, drain well.

◇ Soak sweetbreads in several changes of cold water for 2 hours. Cover with cold water, add the lemon juice and simmer for 5 minutes. Plunge into cold water, gently pull away membrane, then pat dry.

◇ Cut the sweetbreads into small escalopes about 5 mm (¼ inch) thick. Season with salt and pepper and fry in 40 g (1½ oz/3 tbsp) of the butter in a frying pan. At the same time, melt the remaining butter in another frying pan and fry the rhubarb gently, with the sugar, until lightly coloured.

◇ Place the sweetbreads and rhubarb in a heated serving dish and keep warm.

◇ Deglaze the sweetbreads pan with the vinegars. Scrape the base of the pan well with a wooden spatula and allow the juices to reduce slightly while the alcohol evaporates.

◇ Coat sweetbreads with pan juices. Serve immediately.

INGREDIENTS

200 g (7 oz) rhubarb
425 g (15 oz) sweetbreads
juice of ½ lemon
pepper
65 g (2½ oz/5 tbsp) butter
a pinch of sugar
45 ml (3 tbsp) sherry vinegar
45 ml (3 tbsp) red wine vinegar

MAIN COURSE

SERVES 4
Preparation: 15 minutes
Cooking: 10 minutes
Difficulty: **
Cost: **

UTENSILS

1 saucepan
2 frying pans
1 bowl
1 wooden spatula

◇ Peel the rhubarb, cut it into chunks and put it into a bowl with a handful of sea salt. Leave to degorge for about 10 minutes. Rinse well, then blanch in boiling water for 4–5 minutes. Drain the rhubarb, reduce to a purée in a blender or food processor, then sieve.

◇ Heat the oven to 170°C (325°F/Gas Mark 3).

◇ Add the chives, parsley, tarragon, egg yolks, egg and cream to the rhubarb purée. Season with salt and pepper and mix well.

◇ Pour the purée into 6 ramekins. Place them in a bain-marie, cover with foil and bake for 35–45 minutes, until set.

◇ Meanwhile, prepare a fresh tomato coulis: Skin and seed the tomatoes. Purée the tomato flesh in a food processor or food mill.

◇ Allow the custards to cool. Spoon a pool of tomato coulis on to each individual serving plate and turn out 2 custards on to each. Decorate with a little chervil or basil.

INGREDIENTS

700 g (1½ lb) rhubarb
coarse sea salt
5 ml (1 tsp) chopped chives
5 ml (1 tsp) chopped parsley
1 tarragon stalk, chopped
2 egg yolks
1 egg
225 ml (8 fl oz/1 cup) double (heavy) cream
pepper
450 g (1 lb) tomatoes
1 chervil or basil sprig

FIRST COURSE

SERVES 6
Preparation: 15 minutes
Cooking: 40–50 minutes
Difficulty: ★
Cost: ★★

UTENSILS

1 large saucepan
1 blender, food processor or food mill
1 fine sieve
8 ramekins
1 roasting pan or shallow ovenproof dish for the bain-marie
kitchen foil
OVEN
170°C (325°F/Gas Mark 3)

◇ Clean and chop the stock vegetables. Put them into a saucepan with the herbs and 400 ml (14 fl oz/1¾ cups) water. Bring to the boil and simmer for about 20 minutes. Strain and allow to cool.

◇ Peel the rhubarb and cut it into 4 cm (1½ inch) lengths. Cut lengthways into strips about 1 cm (½ inch) wide and 2 mm (⅛ inch) thick. Place the rhubarb in a bowl with a handful of sea salt. Leave to degorge for about 10 minutes, then rinse well and drain.

◇ Prepare a court-bouillon by mixing together the wine, vinegar, salt and pepper and 250 ml (9 fl oz) of the vegetable stock. Place the liquid in a shallow flameproof dish large enough to hold the mackerel in a single layer.

◇ Place the dish over the heat and bring to the boil, then simmer for 5 minutes. Add the rhubarb and cook for 5 minutes.

◇ Add the mackerel, making sure that the liquid covers them. Return to the boil. Add the lemon slices. Immediately remove from the heat and allow to cool. When the liquid is cool, the fish will be cooked.

◇ Serve the mackerel with their cooking liquid and the rhubarb.

INGREDIENTS

300 g (10 oz) rhubarb
coarse sea salt
100 ml (4 fl oz/½ cup) dry white wine
100 ml (4 fl oz/½ cup) malt vinegar
pepper
1 lemon, sliced
FOR THE VEGETABLE
STOCK
1 onion
1 shallot
1 small leek
1 carrot
1 celery stalk
1 thyme sprig
1 bay leaf
2 parsley sprigs

MAIN COURSE

SERVES 4
Preparation: 10 minutes
Cooking: 20 minutes
Difficulty: ★
Cost: ★

UTENSILS

1 large saucepan
1 sieve
1 bowl
1 flameproof dish

◇ Clean and chop the stock vegetables. Put them into a saucepan with the herbs and 250 ml (9 fl oz/1⅛ cups) water. Bring to the boil, then simmer for 25 minutes. Strain.

◇ Peel the rhubarb and cut it into 5 cm (2 inch) lengths, then into strips 1 cm (½ inch) wide and 2 mm (⅛ inch) thick. Put the rhubarb into a bowl with a handful of sea salt and leave to degorge for 10 minutes, then rinse, drain and lay out on a tea-towel.

◇ Cut out 4 circles of greaseproof (parchment) paper about 30–35 cm (12–14 inches) in diameter and brush them with oil. Heat the oven to 200°C (400°F/Gas Mark 7).

◇ Place a mullet fillet on each greaseproof circle and add a little rhubarb and a spoonful of stock. Top with chopped tarragon and a sprinkling of salt and pepper, then brush the edge of each circle with beaten egg yolk, and make parcels by folding the edges of the paper over twice.

◇ Place the papillotes on a lightly oiled baking tray and bake for 8–10 minutes.

◇ Slide the papillotes on to heated dinner plates: each guest will open their own parcel. Serve the melted butter, seasoned with a little lemon juice, separately.

INGREDIENTS

250 g (9 oz) rhubarb
coarse sea salt
groundnut (peanut) oil
4 red mullet fillets
tarragon
pepper
1 egg yolk
50 g (2 oz/4 tbsp) butter, melted
a little lemon juice
FOR THE VEGETABLE
STOCK
½ onion
1 shallot
½ small leek
1 carrot
1 small celery stalk
1 thyme sprig
1 bay leaf
1 parsley sprig

MAIN COURSE

SERVES 4
Preparation: 15 minutes
Cooking: 10–12 minutes
Difficulty: ★★
Cost: ★★

UTENSILS

1 saucepan
greaseproof (parchment) paper
1 baking tray
1 sieve
OVEN
200°C (400°F/Gas Mark 6)

◇ Clean and chop the stock vegetables. Put them into a saucepan with the herbs and 600 ml (1 pint/2½ cups) water. Bring to the boil, then simmer for 20 minutes. Strain.

◇ Meanwhile, peel the rhubarb, cut it into chunks and put it into a bowl with a handful of sea salt. Leave to degorge for 10 minutes, then rinse well and drain.

◇ Fry the fillets of whiting in the butter in a frying pan for 3 minutes on each side. Remove the whiting from the pan and keep warm.

◇ Place the rhubarb in the same pan, adding a little more butter if necessary. Fry the rhubarb for 1–2 minutes until it colours slightly. Add 100 ml (4 fl oz/½ cup) of the stock with the cream and allow to reduce so that the sauce thickens. Season to taste with salt, pepper and a dash of lemon juice.

◇ Place a whiting fillet on each heated dinner plate, coat with the sauce and sprinkle with a little chopped chervil.

INGREDIENTS

250 g (9 oz) rhubarb
coarse sea salt
4 whiting fillets
20 g (⅔ oz/1½ tbsp) butter
200 ml (7 fl oz/⅞ cup) double (heavy) cream
pepper
a little lemon juice
chervil

FOR THE VEGETABLE STOCK
1 onion
1 shallot
1 small leek
1 carrot
1 celery stalk
1 thyme sprig
1 bay leaf
1 parsley sprig

MAIN COURSE

SERVES 4
Preparation: 10 minutes
Cooking: 10 minutes
Difficulty: ★★
Cost: ★

UTENSILS

1 large saucepan
1 sieve
1 frying pan

◇ Clean and chop the stock vegetables. Put them into a saucepan with the herbs and 450 ml (15 fl oz/1¾ cups) water. Bring to the boil, then simmer for 20 minutes. Strain and allow to cool.

◇ Peel the rhubarb and cut it into 5 cm (2 inch) lengths 2 mm (⅛ inch) thick. Put the rhubarb into a bowl with a handful of sea salt and leave to degorge for 10 minutes, then rinse well and drain.

◇ Bring a saucepan of water to the boil and blanch the rhubarb for 2–3 minutes. Run cold water over the rhubarb, to prevent further cooking, then drain well.

◇ Peel and chop the cucumber. Skin and seed the tomatoes; dice the flesh of half a tomato.

◇ Reduce the remaining tomato flesh to a purée with the rhubarb, cucumber and cream in a blender or food processor. Stir in half the stock and the diced tomato. Chill in the refrigerator.

◇ Serve the gazpacho accompanied by small croûtons.

INGREDIENTS

300 g (10 oz) rhubarb
coarse sea salt
½ cucumber
300 g (10 oz) tomatoes
100 ml (4 fl oz/½ cup) double (heavy) cream
small croûtons
FOR THE VEGETABLE STOCK
1 onion
1 shallot
1 small leek
1 carrot
1 celery stalk
1 thyme sprig
1 bay leaf
1 parsley sprig

FIRST COURSE

SERVES 4
Preparation: 20 minutes
Cooking: 3 minutes
Difficulty: ★
Cost: ★

UTENSILS

2 saucepans
1 sieve
1 bowl
1 blender or food processor

BRASSICAS
•AND•
LEAVES

Cabbage

Brussels Sprouts

Cauliflower

Broccoli

Spinach

Sorrel

◆C A B B A G E◆

THE CABBAGE IS one of the oldest known vegetables in Europe. To the Romans, it was a dish which banished melancholy. Cabbage, either raw or boiled in honey, was also eaten by the Roman aristocracy before banquets, to help them withstand the effects of the alcohol they imbibed. Even today, in some Central European countries, raw cabbage leaves are eaten as a restorative after an excess of vodka.

Cabbage is rich in vitamins, and in minerals such as potassium, calcium, magnesium and sulphur. It is low in calories.

Cabbage has only one small drawback; it contains certain carbohydrates which may ferment and cause flatulence. However, cabbage also has certain beneficial properties; it can act as a remedy for many respiratory problems.

◇ BUYING CABBAGE ◇

There are two main types of cabbage: the tight-packed, round-headed cabbage, which may be white, green or red, and the looser-packed spring cabbage, which may range from pale green to violet-tinged.

Choose cabbage which seems heavy in relation to its size. The colour should be bright and the leaves should squeak when squeezed. If snapped, a really fresh cabbage leaf will 'weep'. Do not forget that a cabbage will lose half its bulk in the cooking.

◇ PREPARING CABBAGE ◇

Cut away the coarse outer leaves and the core. Cut the cabbage into quarters. Wash thoroughly (especially the looser-headed varieties) to get rid of mud, slugs, etc.

◇ COOKING CABBAGE ◇

To blanch cabbage, bring a large saucepan of salted water to the boil. Add the chunks of cabbage and boil for 10–15 minutes according to freshness and size. Many cooks and dietitians believe that cabbage is less indigestible if either double-blanched or finely sliced and sautéed in butter. Cabbage cut into quarters may also be sucessfully braised.

◇ CHEF'S TIP ◇

Add a good-sized chunk of bread to the cabbage water to reduce the cooking smell.

◇ RED CABBAGE SALAD ◇

◇ Cut the cabbage into quarters. Remove the tough stalk. Slice the leaves into strips 1 cm ($\frac{1}{2}$ inch) wide, removing any large ribs. Wash the strips, drain well and sprinkle with salt. Add the vinegar and toss well. Heat the oven to lowest setting.

◇ Put the cabbage into an ovenproof dish and cover with foil. Cook in the oven for 1 hour, to soften it.

◇ Remove the cabbage from the oven, place in a colander and allow to cool.

◇ Mix the oils. Peel the apple and cut it into very thin matchsticks 1 mm ($\frac{1}{16}$ inch) wide.

◇ Mix the cabbage and apple in a salad bowl. Add the oils and toss well before serving.

INGREDIENTS

300 g (10 oz) red cabbage
salt
45 ml (3 tbsp) red wine vinegar
10 ml (2 tsp) walnut oil
100 ml (4 fl oz/$\frac{1}{2}$ cup) groundnut
(peanut) oil
$\frac{1}{2}$ eating apple

FIRST COURSE

SERVES 4
Preparation: 10 minutes
Cooking: 60 minutes
Difficulty: ★
Cost: ★

UTENSILS

1 large knife
1 chopping board
1 ovenproof dish
kitchen foil
1 salad bowl
OVEN
lowest setting

◇ STIR-FRIED GREEN CABBAGE ◇

A pleasant acompaniment to sautéed chicken, roast beef or game.

◇ Cut the cabbage into strips 1 cm (½ inch) wide. Wash and drain well.

◇ Melt the butter in a frying pan with a lid. Add the cabbage, salt and pepper. Cook, covered, for 2 minutes, until the cabbage exudes its liquid.

◇ Remove the lid, raise the heat to high and cook for 5 minutes, stirring and tossing the cabbage constantly, to ensure even cooking and avoid any burning.

◇ Check the seasoning before serving.

INGREDIENTS

1 green cabbage, Savoy type
40 g (1½oz/3 tbsp) butter
salt and pepper

SIDE DISH

SERVES 4
Preparation: 5 minutes
Cooking: 10 minutes
Difficulty: *
Cost: *

UTENSILS

1 large frying pan with a lid

◇ RED CABBAGE SALAD WITH LARDONS ◇

◇ Cut the cabbage into quarters. Remove any large ribs. Cut the leaves into strips about 1 cm (½ inch) wide. Wash and drain the strips. Sprinkle them with fine salt. Sprinkle with a little of the vinegar and mix well. Heat the oven to 140°C (275°F/Gas Mark 1).

◇ Place the cabbage in an ovenproof dish. Cover with foil and cook in the oven for 1 hour, to soften it.

◇ 10 minutes before the cabbage is cooked, remove the rind from the bacon and cut the bacon into strips. Fry the strips in the butter until very crisp. Drain on kitchen paper. Discard the fat in the frying pan.

◇ Remove the cabbage from the oven. Place it in a colander and allow it to cool slightly, then transfer to a large bowl.

◇ Mix the oils and pour over the cabbage. Toss well to mix, then transfer to individual serving plates. Divide the lardons among the plates.

◇ Return the frying pan to the heat. Add the remaining vinegar and deglaze the pan. Allow the vinegar to reduce by half. Add a few drops of vinegar to each plate and serve.

INGREDIENTS

1 red cabbage, about (300 g (10 oz)
salt
100 ml (4 fl oz/½ cup) red wine vinegar
100 g (4 oz) lean bacon
10 ml (2 tsp) butter
50 ml (2 fl oz/¼ cup) groundnut
(peanut) oil
5 ml (1 tsp) walnut oil

FIRST COURSE

SERVES 4
Preparation: 10 minutes
Cooking: 1 hour
Difficulty: *
Cost: *

UTENSILS

1 large knife
1 chopping board
1 colander
1 large bowl
1 frying pan
OVEN
140°C (275°F/Gas Mark 1)

◇ Wash the cabbage. Cook it for 20 minutes in boiling water, then plunge it into cold water to prevent further cooking. Drain well. Detach the large leaves one by one. (The small central leaves form part of the stuffing mixture.)

◇ Clean and chop the stock vegetables. Add them to 1.7 litres (3 pints/2 quarts) cold water and bring to the boil, then simmer for 20 minutes. Remove and discard the vegetables.

◇ Chop the inner leaves of the cabbage, and the pork. Cut the cooked ham into small dice.

◇ Peel and chop the onion and shallots. Fry them for 2 minutes in the butter. Mix all these stuffing ingredients in a bowl. Add the egg, and the bread soaked in the milk. Season to taste with salt and pepper.

◇ Line a mixing bowl with a clean tea-towel. Put strips of bacon around the edge of the bowl. Begin to reconstitute the cabbage in the bowl, starting with the largest outer leaves. Spread each leaf with the stuffing mixture before you replace it and pack more stuffing between each layer of cabbage leaves.

◇ When the cabbage is entirely reconstituted, close up the tea-towel around it to form a small bundle. Tie the top securely with string.

◇ Return the vegetable stock to the boil again. Lower the cabbage parcel into it and simmer very gently for 2 hours.

◇ Unwrap the tea-towel very carefully. Place the cabbage in a shallow dish or bowl.

◇ Reduce a little of the stock over a high heat. Add salt and pepper and serve in a sauceboat, to accompany the cabbage.

INGREDIENTS

1 large green cabbage
300 g (10 oz) bacon
400 g (14 oz) boned shoulder of pork
300 g (10 oz) cooked ham
200 g (7 oz) onions
75 g (3 oz) shallots
40 g (1½ oz/3 tbsp) butter
1 egg
50 g (2 oz/1 cup) fresh breadcrumbs
150 ml (5 fl oz/⅔ cup) milk
salt and pepper
FOR THE VEGETABLE STOCK
1 onion
2 carrots
1 leek
2 tomatoes
salt and pepper

MAIN COURSE

SERVES 6
Preparation: 30 minutes
Cooking: 2 hours
Difficulty: **
Cost: *

UTENSILS

1 large saucepan
2 mixing bowls
1 tea-towel

◇ STIR-FRIED GREEN CABBAGE WITH SMOKED HADDOCK AND TARRAGON BUTTER ◇

◇ To make the tarragon butter sauce, which should not be prepared more than 30 minutes in advance, first allow 75 g (3 oz/6 tbsp) of the butter to soften at room temperature.

◇ Put the vinegar, wine, peeled and finely chopped shallots and a pinch of salt into a small saucepan. Reduce over a high heat until the liquid is almost entirely evaporated.

◇ Add the cream and allow it to reduce. Lower heat and whisk in butter a little at a time, until sauce emulsifies.

◇ Cut the cabbage into quarters. Separate the leaves, remove any large ribs and cut the leaves into strips about 1 cm ($\frac{1}{2}$ inch) wide. Wash and drain the cabbage and dry it in a tea-towel.

◇ Melt the remaining butter in a frying pan with a lid. Add the cabbage and cook, covered, for 2 minutes so that the cabbage exudes some of its liquid. Remove the lid and cook the cabbage for a further 5 minutes, stirring.

◇ Meanwhile, put the milk and 200 ml (7 fl oz/$\frac{7}{8}$ cup) water into a saucepan and bring to the boil. Add the haddock and simmer very gently for 5 minutes. Remove and drain; flake into small pieces.

◇ Arrange the cabbage on individual heated dinner plates. Divide the haddock among the plates, coat with the tarragon butter sauce and serve.

INGREDIENTS

100 g (4 oz/1 stick) butter
50 ml (2 fl oz/$\frac{1}{4}$ cup) sherry vinegar
50 ml (2 fl oz/$\frac{1}{4}$ cup) dry white wine
2 small shallots
10 ml (2 tsp) double (heavy) cream
1 green cabbage
100 ml (4 fl oz/$\frac{1}{2}$ cup) milk
300 g (10 oz) smoked haddock

MAIN COURSE

SERVES 4
Preparation: 10 minutes
Cooking: 15 minutes
Difficulty: ★★
Cost: ★★

UTENSILS

1 frying pan with a lid
1 saucepan
1 small saucepan
1 balloon whisk

◇ RED CABBAGE WITH VINEGAR ◇

◇ Cut the cabbage into quarters. Remove any large ribs. Cut the leaves into strips about 1 cm ($\frac{1}{2}$ inch) wide. Wash and drain the strips and dry them in a tea-towel. Put them into a salad bowl.

◇ Put the vinegars into a small saucepan. Bring to the boil and allow to reduce by one-quarter.

◇ Add salt and pepper to the hot vinegar then pour it over the cabbage. The contrast between the hot dressing and the cold crisp cabbage is one of the principal attractions of this dish, so it is vital to serve it immediately.

INGREDIENTS

1 red cabbage, about 300 g (10 oz)
100 ml (4 fl oz/$\frac{1}{2}$ cup) red wine vinegar
50 ml (2 fl oz/$\frac{1}{4}$ cup) sherry vinegar
salt and pepper

FIRST COURSE

SERVES 4
Preparation: 10 minutes
Cooking time: 5 minutes
Difficulty: ★
Cost: ★

UTENSILS

1 large knife
1 chopping board
1 small saucepan
1 salad bowl

·BRUSSELS· SPROUTS

THE BELGIANS CLAIM that this member of the cabbage family was introduced to their country by the Romans, and indeed Pliny mentions the shoots of some type of cabbage; however, it is not clear whether he was referring to some ancestor of the Brussels sprout, or of broccoli.

This smaller relative of the Savoy cabbage shares the characteristics of its cousin, though its taste is perhaps more pronounced and piquant.

◇ BUYING BRUSSELS SPROUTS ◇

Look for small, firm, tightly-furled sprouts with no yellowing leaves. Avoid those which vary greatly in size, since this would complicate timing their cooking.

◇ PREPARING BRUSSELS SPROUTS ◇

Remove any yellowing leaves. Cut away any protruding stalk, leaving 1 mm ($\frac{1}{16}$ inch) to ensure that the outer leaves will not break off during cooking. Blanch the sprouts in boiling water.

◇ COOKING AND SERVING BRUSSELS SPROUTS ◇

After the initial blanching, cook the sprouts in boiling water. Calculate the cooking time from when the pan returns to the boil. Allow 10–15 minutes; if the sprouts are overcooked, they will be unpleasantly mushy.

Do not leave Brussels sprouts to keep warm in their own cooking water; this will make them turn yellow.

Serve Brussels sprouts with game, poultry and pork. They are also excellent cooked with chestnuts.

◇ SAUTEED BRUSSELS SPROUTS ◇

Suitable to serve with roast beef or boeuf à la mode.

◇ Wash and trim the sprouts, then blanch and cook them as described on page 81. Drain well.

◇ Peel and thinly slice the onion. Melt the butter in a frying pan and cook the onion gently until transparent. Add the sprouts and raise the heat. Fry, turning the sprouts until they are lightly coloured.

◇ Sprinkle the sprouts with parsley and serve immediately.

INGREDIENTS

800 g (1¾ lb) sprouts
½ medium onion
50 g (2 oz/4 tbsp) butter
chopped parsley

SIDE DISH

SERVES 4
Preparation: 5 minutes
Cooking: 20–30 minutes
Difficulty: ★
Cost: ★

UTENSILS

1 large frying pan
1 large saucepan

◇ BRUSSELS SPROUTS WITH LARDONS ◇

Serve with rabbit in mustard sauce, roast veal or pork.

◇ Wash and trim the sprouts, then blanch them as described on page 81. Cook them in a fresh pan of boiling salted water for 10–15 minutes.

◇ Meanwhile, remove the rind from the bacon and cut the bacon crossways into matchstick lengths. Fry the bacon strips in a little oil until crisp. Drain on kitchen paper.

◇ Drain the sprouts and refresh in cold water. Drain again. Melt the butter in a frying pan and fry the sprouts until lightly coloured.

◇ Place the sprouts in a heated serving dish. Sprinkle them with the lardons and serve.

INGREDIENTS

550 g (1¼ lb) Brussels sprouts
salt
about 75 g (3 oz) thickly sliced lean
bacon
a little oil
20 g (¾ oz/1½ tbsp) butter

SIDE DISH

SERVES 4
Preparation: 5–10 minutes
Cooking: 20–30 minutes
Difficulty: ★
Cost: ★

UTENSILS

1 large saucepan
1 large frying pan
1 small frying pan
kitchen paper

◇ BRUSSELS SPROUTS IN CREAM ◇

◇ Wash and trim the sprouts, then blanch them as described on page 81. Refresh under cold water, then cook them in a fresh pan of boiling salted water for 10–15 minutes. Drain well.

◇ Meanwhile, heat the butter in a saucepan until nut-brown. Add the drained sprouts and cook for 2 minutes over a high heat, so that they exude some of their liquid. Add the cream to the pan and season with salt and pepper. Bring to the boil and cook for 5–10 minutes before serving.

INGREDIENTS

900 g (2 lb) Brussels sprouts
salt
50 g (2 oz) butter
300 ml (10 fl oz/1¼ cups) double (heavy) cream
pepper

FIRST COURSE

SERVES 4–6
Preparation: 5 minutes
Cooking: 30–35 minutes
Difficulty: ★
Cost: ★

UTENSILS

2 large saucepans

◇ BRAISED BRUSSELS SPROUTS ◇

Serve with roast veal or roast guinea fowl.

◇ Wash and trim the sprouts, then blanch them as described on page 81. Cook them in a fresh pan of boiling salted water for about 12 minutes.

◇ Heat the oven to 180°C (350°F/Gas Mark 4).

◇ Drain the sprouts well. Place them in an ovenproof dish and dot with the butter. Season with salt and pepper.

◇ Cover with foil and cook in the oven until the sprouts are tender when tested with the point of a knife.

INGREDIENTS

900 g (2 lb) Brussels sprouts
salt
50 g (2 oz/4 tbsp) butter

SIDE DISH

SERVES 4–6
Preparation: 5 minutes
Cooking: 30–35 minutes
Difficulty: ★
Cost: ★

UTENSILS

1 large saucepan
1 ovenproof dish
kitchen foil
OVEN
180°C (350°F/Gas Mark 4)

◇ BRUSSELS SPROUTS WITH PIQUANT HOLLANDAISE SAUCE ◇

◇ Wash and trim the sprouts, then blanch them as described on page 81. Cook them in a fresh pan of boiling salted water for 10–15 minutes. Drain the sprouts well.

◇ While the sprouts are cooking, prepare the sauce. Place the vinegars in a small saucepan. Boil the mixture to reduce by three-quarters.

◇ Remove the pan from the heat. Add 50 ml (2 fl oz/$\frac{1}{4}$ cup) cold water and the egg yolks. Beat vigorously with a balloon whisk. As soon as the sauce begins to form, return the pan to a very gentle heat. Continue to whisk until the sauce reaches the consistency of mayonnaise. (Be very careful not to overheat the mixture as the yolks must on no account curdle.) Whisk in the clarified butter.

◇ Sprinkle the sprouts with chopped parsley and serve accompanied by the sauce in a sauceboat.

INGREDIENTS

550 g (1$\frac{1}{4}$ lb) Brussels sprouts
salt
100 ml (4 fl oz/$\frac{1}{2}$ cup) red wine vinegar
100 ml (4 fl oz/$\frac{1}{2}$ cup) sherry vinegar
2 egg yolks
150 g (5 oz/1$\frac{1}{4}$ sticks) butter, clarified
1 small bunch of parsley

FIRST COURSE

SERVES 4
Preparation: 10–35 minutes
Cooking: 20–30 minutes
Difficulty: ★★★
Cost: ★

UTENSILS

2 small saucepans
1 large saucepan

◆ CAULIFLOWER ◆

THE CAULIFLOWER, a relative of the cabbage, has been known for several thousand years in Syria, Turkey and Egypt. It was introduced to Spain in the twelfth century, but did not reach England and France until the end of the sixteenth century.

◇ BUYING CAULIFLOWER ◇

The florets must be white and closely packed, and the surrounding leaves crisp. Avoid any cauliflowers which have yellowed florets or which show signs of bolting.

◇ PREPARING CAULIFLOWER ◇

Cut away the outer leaves. Trim the stalk so that the cauliflower stands level. Trim away any damaged florets. Hollow out the central stalk to a depth of 5 cm (2 inches).

◇ COOKING AND SERVING CAULIFLOWER ◇

Put 2.5 cm (1 inch) water into a large saucepan. Add salt and bring to the boil. Add the cauliflower, base downwards. Return to the boil. Cover the pan tightly and cook for 15 minutes over a high heat. (Allow a little longer if the cauliflower is very large.) In this manner, the stalk cooks in the boiling water while the florets steam. Remove and drain the cauliflower.

Serve cauliflower with meat, fish and egg dishes.

◇ CHEF'S TIP ◇

Cauliflower is not suitable for cooking in a pressure cooker, as it will discolour.

◇ Separate the cauliflower into individual florets and wash them. Bring a large pan of salted water to the boil. Cook the florets for 4–5 minutes. Drain the cauliflower in a colander, then on a tea-towel.

◇ Trim away the lower part of the watercress stalks. Bring another saucepan of salted water to the boil. Reserve a few watercress leaves to garnish and blanch the remainder for 5 minutes. Drain, then refresh in iced water. Drain the watercress very thoroughly and chop it finely, preferably in a food processor.

◇ Place the cream in a small saucepan and boil it to reduce by one-quarter.

◇ Heat half the butter in a medium saucepan, until lightly browned. Add the chopped watercress and the reduced cream. Season to taste with salt and pepper. Mix well. As soon as the purée has absorbed all the butter, reduce the heat to low and cover.

◇ Melt the remaining butter in a frying pan. Heat the cauliflower florets in it gently. Take care not to break the florets when turning them.

◇ Pour the watercress purée into a heated serving dish. Arrange the cauliflower florets on it and garnish with the reserved watercress leaves.

INGREDIENTS

1 cauliflower
salt
2 bunches of watercress
200 ml (7 fl oz/⅞ cup) double cream
75 g (3 oz/6 tbsp) butter
salt and pepper

FIRST COURSE

SERVES 4
Preparation time: 10 minutes
Cooking time: 10 minutes
Difficulty: ★
Cost: ★

UTENSILS

1 large saucepan
2 medium saucepans
1 small saucepan
1 food processor
1 large colander
1 frying pan

◇ CAULIFLOWER CANAPES ◇

◇ Divide the cauliflower into small florets. Wash and drain well.
◇ If the anchovy fillets are large, halve them lengthways. Wind a fillet around the stem of each floret and secure with a cocktail stick (toothpick).

INGREDIENTS

1 medium cauliflower
1 can of anchovy fillets

COCKTAIL SNACK

SERVES 4–6
Preparation: 5–10 minutes
Difficulty: ★
Cost: ★

UTENSILS

cocktail sticks (toothpicks)

◇ CAULIFLOWER AND CORIANDER SALAD ◇

◇ Divide the cauliflower into small florets. Wash and drain them well.
◇ Make a dressing by mixing together the olive oil, lemon juice, coriander seeds, salt and pepper in a large bowl.
◇ Toss the cauliflower florets in the dressing. Place them in a salad bowl and sprinkle with chopped coriander.

INGREDIENTS

1 cauliflower
150 ml (5 fl oz/⅔ cup) olive oil
juice of 1 lemon
15 ml (1 tbsp) coriander seeds, crushed
salt and white pepper
1 small bunch of fresh coriander

FIRST COURSE

SERVES 4
Preparation: 5 minutes
Difficulty: ★
Cost: ★

UTENSILS

1 large bowl
1 salad bowl

◇ CAULIFLOWER WITH A COULIS OF RED AND GREEN PEPPERS ◇

◇ Separate the cauliflower into small florets and wash them. Bring a large saucepan of salted water to the boil. Cook the cauliflower florets for 4–5 minutes. Drain them in a colander and leave to dry on a tea-towel.

◇ Cut the peppers in half lengthways and remove the stalks and seeds. Cut the peppers into strips. Heat the olive oil in a frying pan with a lid. Add the peeled and finely chopped shallot and the pepper strips. Cover and cook over a gentle heat for 8 minutes, then add the cream, salt and pepper. Lower the heat and cook uncovered for 5 minutes. Reduce to a purée in a food processor or blender.

◇ Wash the beans, then top and tail them. Bring a saucepan of lightly salted water to the boil. Cook the beans for 6–8 minutes, then drain. Refresh under cold water and drain again thoroughly.

◇ Seed the peppers for the garnish and cut them into matchstick lengths. Plunge them into boiling water for 2–3 minutes, then drain.

◇ Reheat the cauliflower gently in half the butter. Season with salt and pepper.

◇ In another saucepan, reheat the French beans in the remaining way. Season with salt and pepper.

◇ Pour a pool of the pepper coulis on to each individual serving plate. Arrange cauliflower florets in the centre; arrange the beans around the edge of the plates. Garnish with the julienne of peppers.

INGREDIENTS

1 cauliflower

salt

50 g (2 oz) red sweet pepper

50 g (2 oz) green sweet pepper

10 ml (2 tsp) olive oil

1 shallot

100 ml (4 fl oz/½ cup) double (heavy) cream

pepper

100 g (4 oz) French (green) beans

50 g (2 oz/4 tbsp) butter

TO GARNISH

¼ red sweet pepper

¼ green sweet pepper

FIRST COURSE

SERVES 4

Preparation: 10 minutes

Cooking: 15 minutes

Difficulty: ★★

Cost: ★

UTENSILS

1 large saucepan

1 chopping board

1 frying pan

1 food processor or blender

2 medium saucepans

1 colander

◆ B R O C C O L I ◆

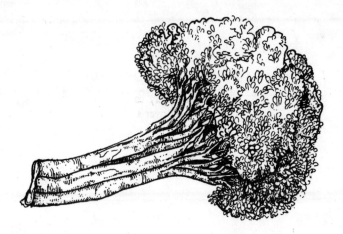

Broccoli, described by Pliny as an exceptional vegetable, is coming back into vogue. Because of its attractive colour, it is often used as a garnish; its springlike green looks most attractive offsetting a creamy sauce. But broccoli should not be neglected as a valuable foodstuff in its own right. It is rich in Vitamins A, C and folic acid as well as minerals potassium, calcium, magnesium and iron.

There are two types of broccoli; green calabrese, which has a more delicate flavour, and white or purple sprouting broccoli, found in many vegetable gardens and country markets.

◇ BUYING BROCCOLI ◇

Select calabrese of a good strong green colour; avoid any which is yellowed. Purple and white sprouting broccoli should be crisp and firm.

Use the whole head and stalks. Small florets of calabrese are preferable for use as a garnish or when making a gratin. Allow 200 g (7 oz) per person.

◇ PREPARING BROCCOLI ◇

Tear off any small leaves. With a sharp knife, peel away the outer skin which covers the stalks, working away from the head. Cut the heads away from the main stalk. Cut the stalks into halves or quarters, depending on their thickness, and then into pieces about 1 cm ($\frac{1}{2}$ inch) long. This will ensure that the stalks cook at the same speed as the heads.

Like all green vegetables, broccoli will regain some of its freshness and have a better colour if it is soaked in cold water for a few minutes before preparation.

◇ COOKING BROCCOLI ◇

Broccoli is best if steamed, or boiled, uncovered, for a few minutes. Cooking time should be very short. Plunge the cooked broccoli into iced water to prevent further cooking and preserve the colour. If cooked and refreshed in this way, then reheated in a steamer while you are serving up the rest of the dish, broccoli will look and taste its best. Any left-over broccoli may be made into an excellent creamed soup.

◇ FREEZING BROCCOLI ◇

Broccoli freezes well. Blanch individual florets or the entire head for 1 minute, then plunge it into ice-cold water. Drain well and allow to cool on a wire tray before packing into freezer bags.

◇ WARM SALAD OF BROCCOLI AND TOMATOES ◇

◇ Prepare the broccoli as described on page 89. Cook it in boiling salted water for 5–7 minutes. Remove the broccoli with a slotted spoon (reserve the cooking water) and plunge into iced water. Drain well.

◇ Skin and seed the tomatoes. Cut the flesh into small dice.

◇ Wash the salad leaves and dry well. Prepare the vinaigrette by mixing together all the ingredients.

◇ Put the salad leaves into a serving bowl. Add a little of the vinaigrette and toss well. Re-heat the cooking water. Then warm the broccoli slightly in the water, or by steaming it over the water.

◇ Mix the warmed broccoli with the diced tomato and the rest of the vinaigrette. Arrange this mixture on top of the salad and serve immediately.

INGREDIENTS

1.1 kg (2¼ lb) broccoli
salt
200 g (7 oz) ripe tomatoes
100 g (4 oz) salad leaves, preferably rocket or mesclun

FOR THE VINAIGRETTE
20 ml (4 tsp) wine vinegar
10 ml (2 tsp) sherry vinegar
30 ml (2 tbsp) grapeseed or vegetable oil
1.25 ml (¼ tsp) prepared mustard
1 small shallot, finely chopped
salt and pepper

FIRST COURSE

SERVES 4
Preparation: 10 minutes
Cooking: 10 minutes
Difficulty: *
Cost: *

UTENSILS

1 large saucepan
1 small bowl
1 salad bowl

◇ BROCCOLI FRIED IN BUTTER ◇

This is an excellent accompaniment to roast meat.

◇ Prepare the broccoli as described on page 89. Cook in boiling salted water for 4–5 minutes. Remove the broccoli with a slotted spoon and plunge into iced water. In view of the second cooking it will undergo, take care not to overcook the broccoli at this stage.

◇ Drain the broccoli well. Melt the butter in a frying pan and fry the broccoli gently. It should not brown or become crisp. Season the broccoli with salt and pepper, and garnish with chervil sprigs.

INGREDIENTS

1.1 kg (2¼ lb) broccoli
salt
25 g (1 oz/2 tbsp) butter
pepper
1 small bunch of chervil

SIDE DISH

SERVES 4
Preparation: 10 minutes
Cooking: 10 minutes
Difficulty: ★
Cost: ★

UTENSILS

1 large saucepan
1 frying pan

◇ BROCCOLI PUREE ◇

◇ Prepare the broccoli as described on page 89. Cook in boiling salted water for 3–4 minutes. Remove the broccoli and drain thoroughly. Reduce to a purée in a blender or food processor, then sieve to make a smooth purée.

◇ Bring the cream to the boil in a saucepan. Allow it to reduce and thicken.

◇ Melt the butter in another saucepan. Allow it to brown but be careful it does not burn. Without removing the pan from the heat, add the broccoli purée. Beat vigorously with a wooden spoon. Then, with the pan still over the heat, add the cream. Beat well to mix. Season to taste with salt and pepper and serve very hot.

INGREDIENTS

1.4 kg (3 lb) broccoli
150 ml (5 fl oz/⅔ cup) double (heavy) cream
25 g (1 oz/2 tbsp) butter
salt and pepper

SIDE DISH

SERVES 6
Preparation: 10 minutes
Cooking: 10 minutes
Difficulty: ★
Cost: ★

UTENSILS

1 large saucepan
1 blender or food processor
2 small saucepans
1 sieve
1 wooden spoon

◇ Prepare the broccoli as described on page 89.

◇ Bring a large saucepan of salted water to the boil. Cook the broccoli for 4–5 minutes. Remove with a slotted spoon and immediately plunge into iced water. Drain and set aside, reserving the cooking water.

◇ Clean and roughly chop the stock vegetables. Put into a saucepan with 300 ml (10 fl oz/1¼ cups) cold water. Bring to the boil. Cover and cook for 20 minutes.

◇ To make the sauce, put the vinegars and peppercorns into a small saucepan. Boil until the liquid has almost entirely evaporated. Add 100 ml (4 fl oz/½ cup) of the vegetable stock. Cook for 5 minutes, then strain through a fine sieve into a *cold* saucepan.

◇ Add the egg yolks and whisk to blend well over lowest possible heat, or in a bain-marie. Whisk in the clarified butter and lemon juice, and season the sauce to taste with salt and pepper.

◇ Pour a pool of the sauce on to each heated individual serving plate. Warm the broccoli slightly by returning it to its reheated cooking water for 1 minute. Drain well on kitchen paper. Divide between the plates. Garnish with chervil sprigs and serve.

INGREDIENTS

1.4 kg (3 lb) broccoli
salt
30 ml (2 tbsp) red wine vinegar
30 ml (2 tbsp) sherry vinegar
5 ml (1 tsp) crushed peppercorns
2 egg yolks
100 g (4 oz/1 stick) butter, clarified
5 ml (1 tsp) lemon juice
pepper
1 bunch of chervil
FOR THE VEGETABLE STOCK
1 carrot
½ onion
½ leek

FIRST COURSE

SERVES 6
Preparation: 10 minutes
Cooking: 15 minutes
Difficulty: ★★★
Cost: ★

UTENSILS

1 large saucepan
3 small saucepans
1 fine sieve
1 balloon whisk

•S P I N A C H•

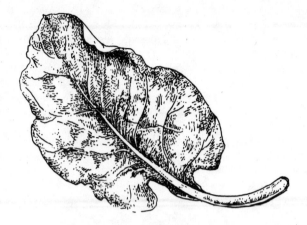

Spinach originated in either Asia Minor or the Far East, but neither region has yet proved its claim conclusively. It was not until the end of the Middle Ages that the Arabs introduced spinach to Europe. They did so in the belief that it provided a most beneficial poultice for the liver and the stomach!

By the end of the nineteenth century, spinach was regarded as a plant with near-miraculous properties: because of its high iron content it was thought of as a tonic. Today, these benefits are considered to be offset by a serious drawback; the presence in spinach of toxic nitrites, products of heavy use of chemical fertilizers.

However, spinach is still rich in Vitamins A, B (folic acid) and C, in iron, calcium and magnesium. But its levels of oxalate mean that spinach should be avoided by those suffering from kidney stones.

Spinach is a vegetable which does not thrive in dry conditions, when its level of oxalate increases and it goes to seed. It can be eaten raw or cooked, but must be used as soon as possible after cooking.

◇ BUYING SPINACH ◇

Look for healthy, unspotted leaves. The exact colour will depend on variety, but the lighter, thinner spring spinach is better for salads; the thicker autumn and winter spinach cooks better.

Allow 450 g (1 lb) per person if the finished dish is to be the only accompaniment to a main course. The removal of the stalks and the loss of volume during cooking account for the seemingly large quantity. Allow 100 g (4 oz) per person if the spinach is to be served raw in a salad.

◇ PREPARING SPINACH ◇

Check each leaf individually. Strip away the central stalk, unless the leaf is very small and tender. Wash the leaves in several changes of cold water, to remove all soil and grit.

◇ COOKING AND SERVING SPINACH ◇

Spinach should first be cooked in well-salted boiling water. The leaves should then be plunged into cold water to remove the salt and prevent further cooking. After thorough draining, the spinach should be reheated in butter.

For tender leaves, bring 1 cm ($\frac{1}{2}$ inch) salted water to the boil. Add the spinach. Do not cover as this would make the leaves turn yellow. As soon as the leaves begin to wilt, transfer them to a bowl of iced water. Drain well.

For thicker leaves (especially the autumn and winter varieties), bring 1 litre ($1\frac{3}{4}$ pints/1 quart) water to the boil with 10 ml (2 tsp) salt. Add the spinach, return to the boil, then cook for 2–5 minutes. Transfer the leaves to a bowl of iced water. Drain and squeeze the leaves between your hands, to extract as much water as possible.

Spinach requires large quantities of butter, if it is to be really succulent. For most recipes, sauté the leaves for 2 minutes in *beurre noisette* (lightly browned butter, see Gratin of Spinach and Mushroom, page 95). The flavour will be enhanced if you impale a clove of garlic on a fork and use it to stir the spinach as it cooks. Be sure to remove the garlic before serving.

Serve with meat dishes, eggs and cheese.

◇ SPINACH SALAD WITH LARDONS ◇

◇ Wash and trim the spinach. Drain the leaves well.

◇ Remove the bacon rind and cut the bacon into small dice. Put into a small saucepan of cold water and bring to the boil. Skim off the surface scum, then drain.

◇ Heat the 10 ml (2 tsp) groundnut oil in a frying pan and fry the lardons until browned. Drain them on kitchen paper, to remove as much oil as possible.

◇ To make the vinaigrette, mix together the ingredients in the listed order.

◇ Just before serving heat the oven to 180°C (350°F/Gas Mark 4). Place the spinach and lardons in a heatproof salad bowl. Whisk the vinaigrette, pour it over the spinach leaves and toss well. Put the bowl into the oven for 3 minutes, to warm it slightly.

INGREDIENTS

450 g (1 lb) young, tender spinach
200 g (7 oz) bacon
10 ml (2 tsp) groundnut (peanut) oil
FOR THE VINAIGRETTE
10 ml (2 tsp) wine vinegar
10 ml (2 tsp) sherry vinegar
salt and pepper
1 shallot, peeled and finely chopped
5 ml (1 tsp) strong prepared mustard
5 ml (1 tsp) walnut oil
10 ml (2 tsp) groundnut (peanut) oil

FIRST COURSE

SERVES 4
Preparation: 12 minutes
Cooking: 5 minutes
Difficulty: ★
Cost: ★

UTENSILS

1 heatproof salad bowl
1 small frying pan
1 small saucepan
kitchen paper
OVEN
180°C (350°F/Gas Mark 4)

Buttery spinach covered with a layer of mushrooms and topped with mushroom-flavoured cream is quickly browned in a hot oven.

◇ Wash and trim the spinach. Cook it, uncovered, in boiling water, then drain, as described on page 94.

◇ Meanwhile, prepare the mushrooms. Trim the stalks, wash the mushroom caps and slice thinly (about 2 mm (⅛ inch) thick). Add the lemon juice, to prevent the mushrooms from discolouring.

◇ Fry the mushrooms in 15 g (½ oz/1 tbsp) of the butter over a moderate heat, until they exude their liquid. Put them to drain in a colander set over a bowl. When the mushrooms are thoroughly drained, put the liquid into a small saucepan and boil to reduce by half.

◇ Meanwhile, pour the cream into the pan in which you cooked the mushrooms and allow it to reduce. When it is smooth and thick, return the mushrooms and their reduced liquid to the pan and cook for 2 minutes.

◇ Prepare a *beurre noisette* by melting the remaining butter in a sauté pan, taking care that it does not burn. Keep it over a low heat and skim away the foam that forms, until the butter turns an attractive nut-brown.

◇ Cook the spinach in the *beurre noisette*, stirring the contents of the pan with the garlic clove impaled on a fork, for extra flavour. Season to taste with salt and pepper.

◇ Heat the oven to its highest setting.

◇ Place the spinach in a buttered gratin dish. Spread the mushrooms and cream mixture evenly on top. Place in the oven for a few minutes, so that the topping colours slightly.

INGREDIENTS

1.1 kg (2½ lb) spinach
200 g (7 oz) mushrooms
juice of ½ lemon
115 g (4½ oz/9 tbsp) butter
250 ml (9 fl oz/1 cup) double (heavy) cream
1 garlic clove
salt and pepper

SIDE DISH

SERVES 4–6
Preparation: 15 minutes
Cooking: 12 minutes
Difficulty: *
Cost: **

UTENSILS

1 large saucepan
1 sauté pan
1 gratin dish
1 frying pan
1 colander
1 small saucepan
OVEN
240°C (475°F/Gas Mark 9)

◇ SPINACH SALAD WITH DOUBLE VINAIGRETTE ◇

◇ Wash and trim the spinach. Drain the leaves well.

◇ Melt the butter in a small frying pan. Fry the chicken liver for a few seconds on each side. Transfer the contents of the pan to a bowl and mash well with a fork.

◇ To make the vinaigrette, mix the ingredients in the listed order, adding the mashed chicken liver before the oils.

◇ Heat the oven to 180° (350°F/Gas Mark 4).

◇ Just before serving, put the spinach into a heatproof salad bowl. Whisk the vinaigrette, pour it over the spinach leaves and toss well. Put the bowl into the oven for 3 minutes, to warm it slightly.

INGREDIENTS

450 g (1 lb) young, tender spinach
15 g ($\frac{1}{2}$ oz/1 tbsp) butter
1 chicken liver
FOR THE VINAIGRETTE
10 ml (2 tsp) wine vinegar
10 ml (2 tsp) sherry vinegar
1 shallot, peeled and finely chopped
5 ml (1 tsp) strong prepared mustard
30 ml (2 tbsp) groundnut (peanut) oil
5 ml (1 tsp) walnut oil

FIRST COURSE

SERVES 4
Preparation: 10 minutes
Cooking: 5 minutes
Difficulty: ★
Cost: ★

UTENSILS

1 heatproof salad bowl
1 small bowl
1 small frying pan
OVEN
180°C (350°F/Gas Mark 4)

◇ BUTTERED SPINACH ◇

This goes very well with veal escalopes.

◇ Wash and trim the spinach. Cook it, uncovered, in boiling water, then drain as described on page 94.

◇ Remove the crusts from the bread and cut the bread into small cubes. Fry in half the butter until crisp, then drain well on kitchen paper.

◇ Prepare a *beurre noisette* by melting the remaining butter in a sauté pan, taking care that it does not burn. Keep it over a low heat and skim away the foam that forms, until the butter turns an attractive nut-brown.

◇ Sauté the spinach briefly in the *beurre noisette*, stirring with the garlic clove impaled on a fork, for extra flavour.

◇ Pile the spinach into a heated serving dish and serve sprinkled with the croûtons.

INGREDIENTS

900 g (2 lb) spinach
2 thick slices white bread
100 g (4 oz/1 stick) butter
1 garlic clove

SIDE DISH

SERVES 4–6
Preparation: 10 minutes
Cooking: 5 minutes
Difficulty: ★
Cost: ★

UTENSILS

1 large saucepan
1 sauté pan
1 frying pan

◇ SPINACH SALAD WITH CHICKEN LIVERS ◇

◇ Wash and trim the spinach. Drain the leaves well.

◇ Clean the chicken livers, being careful to cut away any greenish parts. Melt the butter in a frying pan and fry the chicken livers to seal and brown slightly – they should still be pink inside. Cut each liver in half and keep warm.

◇ To make the vinaigrette, mix together the ingredients in the listed order.

◇ Just before serving, heat the oven to 180°C (350°F/Gas Mark 4). Place the spinach in a heatproof bowl. Whisk the vinaigrette, pour it over the leaves and toss well. Put the bowl into the oven for 3 minutes, to warm it slightly.

◇ Meanwhile, use the 10 ml (2 tsp) sherry vinegar to deglaze the pan in which the livers were cooked. Scrape the base and sides of the pan well with a wooden spatula and allow the vinegar to reduce almost completely

◇ Place a bed of spinach leaves on each individual serving plate. Arrange 6 chicken liver slices on each and add a little of the pan juices. Serve immediately.

INGREDIENTS

450 g (1 lb) young, tender spinach
8 chicken livers
20 g (¾ oz/1½ tbsp) butter
10 ml (2 tsp) sherry vinegar
FOR THE VINAIGRETTE
10 ml (2 tsp) wine vinegar
10 ml (2 tsp) sherry vinegar
salt and pepper
1 shallot, peeled and finely chopped
5 ml (1 tsp) strong prepared mustard
30 ml (2 tbsp) groundnut (peanut) oil
5 ml (1 tsp) walnut oil

FIRST COURSE

SERVES 4
Preparation: 12 minutes
Cooking: 3 minutes
Difficulty: *
Cost: *

UTENSILS

1 large heatproof bowl
1 small frying pan
1 small bowl
OVEN
180°C (350°F/Gas Mark 4)

97

◇ Heat the oven to 170°C (325°F/Gas Mark 3). Pour water to a depth of 2 cm (¾ inch) into an ovenproof dish or roasting pan, and place some folded newspaper in the base, so that the water does not come to the boil. Place this bain-marie in the oven.

◇ Wash and trim the spinach. Cook it, uncovered, in boiling water, then drain, as described on page 94.

◇ Prepare a *beurre noisette* by melting the remaining butter in a sauté pan, taking care that it does not burn. Keep it over a low heat and skim away the foam that forms, until the butter turns an attractive nut-brown.

◇ Sauté the spinach briefly in the *beurre noisette,* stirring with the garlic clove impaled on a fork, for extra flavour.

◇ Meanwhile, put the cream into a small saucepan and allow it to thicken and reduce over a moderate heat.

◇ Reduce the spinach to a purée in a blender or food processor. Add the cream, egg, extra yolks and lemon juice. Season with salt and pepper and mix well.

◇ Pour the mixture into 8 buttered ramekins and press the mixture down gently with the back of a spoon. Place in the bain-marie, cover with foil and bake in the oven for 30–35 minutes, until the custards are set. Turn out and serve with Fresh Tomato Sauce (page 31).

INGREDIENTS

900 g (2 lb) spinach
50 g (2 oz/4 tbsp) butter
1 garlic clove
200 ml (7 fl oz/⅞ cup) double (heavy) cream
1 egg
2 egg yolks
juice of ½ lemon
salt and pepper

FIRST COURSE OR SIDE DISH

SERVES 4–8
Preparation: 15 minutes
Cooking: 50 minutes – 1 hour
Difficulty: ★
Cost: ★

UTENSILS

1 large saucepan
1 sauté pan
1 ovenproof dish or roasting pan
8 ramekins
1 blender or food processor
kitchen foil
1 small saucepan
OVEN
170°C (325°F/Gas Mark 3)

•S O R R E L•

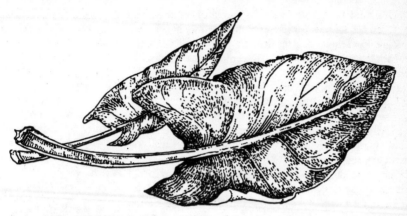

Sorrel originated in northern Asia. It has been in culinary use for only a few hundred years, and it has recently come into vogue with *cuisine nouvelle*. However, the plant's natural acidity and its high levels of oxalic acid make it unsuitable for those afflicted by kidney stones. Among the beneficial properties of sorrel, on the other hand, is said to be the power to cure scurf and boils. It can also be crushed in oil and used to clean silver; sorrel leaves will help remove inkstains from fabric. Sorrel is rich in Vitamins A (carotene) and C as well as minerals potassium, calcium and iron.

◇ *BUYING SORREL* ◇
Look for fresh, unspotted leaves of uniform colour. As with spinach, the level of oxalic acid in sorrel rises quickly once it has been cooked, so sorrel should be used quickly. Remember that its volume diminishes by 75 per cent during cooking.

◇ *PREPARING SORREL* ◇
Wash thoroughly in several changes of water. Remove the stalk by folding the leaf in half lengthways and pulling the stalk backwards.

◇ *COOKING AND SERVING SORREL* ◇
Sorrel is never blanched; instead, it is cooked over a gentle heat, with a little butter or water. It must be stirred constantly.
 Sorrel makes a wonderful sauce to serve with veal, fish and eggs. It also makes superb soup.

◇ *CHEF'S TIPS* ◇
A sorrel purée will be tastier and less acid if you add to it some lettuce, which has a much blander flavour when cooked.
 If you are cooking a fish with particularly fine bones, such as a tail of conger eel, shad, herring, etc., the addition of sorrel will melt away these bones during the cooking process.

◇ Wash and prepare the sorrel as described on page 99. Using kitchen scissors, cut the sorrel into strips 1 cm ($\frac{1}{2}$ inch) wide. Peel and thinly slice the shallots.

◇ Melt the butter in a shallow flameproof casserole and add the tuna, shallots, garlic and thyme. Cook for about 15 minutes, turning the tuna once, until cooked through.

◇ Heat the oven to 100°C (200°F/Gas Mark 1).

◇ Transfer the tuna to a serving platter and put it into the oven to keep warm. Return the casserole to the heat and deglaze with the wine, scraping the base and sides well to loosen any sediment. Allow the liquid to evaporate almost entirely. Add the cream and allow to reduce gently for 5 minutes, until thick and smooth.

◇ Pass the contents of the casserole through a fine sieve into a small saucepan, pressing with the back of a spoon to extract as much flavour as possible. Bring the contents of the pan to the boil and add the sorrel strips. Bring just to the boil, then remove from the heat. Add the lemon juice. Taste the sauce and add salt and pepper if needed.

◇ Serve the sauce in a sauceboat, to accompany the tuna.

INGREDIENTS

50 g (2 oz) sorrel, about 1 small handful

2 shallots

25 g (1 oz/2 tbsp) butter

1 fresh tuna steak, about 800 g (1$\frac{3}{4}$ lb)

1 garlic clove, unpeeled

1 small thyme sprig

100 ml (4 fl oz/$\frac{1}{2}$ cup) dry white wine

200 ml (7 fl oz/$\frac{7}{8}$ cup) double (heavy) cream

juice of $\frac{1}{2}$ lemon

salt and pepper

MAIN COURSE

SERVES 4

Preparation: 10 minutes
Cooking: 20 minutes
Difficulty: ★★
Cost: ★

UTENSILS

1 flameproof casserole
1 small saucepan
1 fine sieve
kitchen scissors
OVEN
100°C (200°F/Gas Mark 1)

The soup may be garnished with crispy fried croûtons, if desired.

◇ Clean the stock vegetables and chop them coarsely. Put them into a saucepan with 600 ml (1 pint) water and the herbs. Bring to the boil, then simmer for 20 minutes. Strain and leave to cool.

◇ Wash and trim the sorrel as described on page 99. Using kitchen scissors, cut it into fine shreds.

◇ Peel and remove the seeds from the pumpkin; cut the flesh into small dice. Melt the butter in a large saucepan and fry the pumpkin gently for a few minutes. Add the stock and cook gently until the pieces of pumpkin can be crushed easily between 2 spoons.

◇ Add the cream to the pan and reduce the mixture to a purée in a blender or food processor. Return it to the pan and return to the boil. Season with salt, pepper and nutmeg. Pour into a heated soup tureen, add the sorrel and serve immediately.

INGREDIENTS

8 sorrel leaves
450 g (1 lb) pumpkin
20 g (¾ oz/1½ tbsp) butter
250 ml (9 fl oz/1 cup) double (heavy) cream
salt and pepper
freshly grated nutmeg

FOR THE VEGETABLE STOCK

1 large onion
2 shallots
1½ leeks
2 carrots
1 celery stalk
1 thyme sprig
1 bay leaf
1 parsley sprig

FIRST COURSE

SERVES 4
Preparation: 10 minutes
Cooking: 20 minutes
Difficulty: ★
Cost: ★

UTENSILS

1 large saucepan
1 blender or food processor

◇ Wash and trim the sorrel as described on page 99. Using kitchen scissors, cut the sorrel into strips about 1 cm ($\frac{1}{2}$ inch) wide.

◇ Grill the sardines until just cooked. Keep hot.

◇ Melt the butter in a saucepan and add the sorrel; leave the pan over the heat just long enough for the sorrel to begin to wilt, but do not allow it to cook.

◇ Remove the pan from the heat, and toss the sorrel in the butter with a fork, without squashing it.

◇ Arrange a bed of sorrel on each heated dinner plate and arrange the sardines on top.

◇ Put the lemon juice, salt and pepper, olive oil and coriander seeds into a bowl and mix well. Coat the sardines and sorrel with the mixture and serve immediately.

INGREDIENTS

100 g (4 oz) sorrel leaves
16–20 fresh sardines
20 g ($\frac{3}{4}$ oz/1$\frac{1}{2}$ tbsp) butter
juice of 1 lemon
salt and pepper
coriander seeds
60 ml (4 tbsp) olive oil

MAIN COURSE

SERVES 4
Preparation: 5 minutes
Cooking: 5 minutes
Difficulty: ★
Cost: ★

UTENSILS

1 large saucepan
1 small bowl

THE ONION
•FAMILY•

•O N I O N S•

T HE ONION IS perhaps the only truly international vegetable, eaten in all corners of the world. It was first grown, and indeed venerated, in Persia. The Egyptians, Greeks and Romans were not slow to recognize its qualities. The Gauls, whose onion crops were much envied by the Romans, believed that onions predicted the weather; the thicker the skins, the harsher the winter ahead.

Two types of onion are generally available. Spring onions, small, young and green, are grown especially for salad use. Mature, larger onions are available throughout the year in a variety of types and sizes: these include the sweet Spanish onion and onions with red skins and red-tinged flesh.

◇ BUYING ONIONS ◇

The stalks of spring onions must be in good condition, with no sign of sliminess, and still firmly attached to the small white bulbs. They should have a strong, clean smell.

Larger onions should be firm and well coloured, with no sign of sprouting. The skins should still be attached, to give the bulb some protection.

◇ CHEF'S TIPS ◇

Eliminate the smell of onions on the breath by chewing a few grains of coffee.

Rub your hands with coarse salt or a cut lemon, and rinse in cold water, after chopping onions.

To prevent onions added whole to a dish from breaking up as they cook, cut a cross in the base.

To avoid weeping as you peel onions, place them in the freezer for 10 minutes, or in the refrigerator for 1 hour, before preparing. Hold them under a gently running tap as you work.

Do not keep half-used raw onions. Once peeled and cut, onions rapidly undergo chemical changes which alter their taste.

◇ GLAZED BABY ONIONS ◇

◇ Peel the onions. Put them into a sauté pan in a single layer. Add enough water to just cover, with the butter, salt and sugar.

◇ Cook, uncovered, over a moderate heat, until the water is completely evaporated, and the onions are tender. Turn the onions from time to time as they cook, so that they are all coated in the buttery juices.

INGREDIENTS

450 g (1 lb) small new season's onions
15 g (½oz/1 tbsp) butter
2 pinches of salt
2 pinches of sugar

SIDE DISH

SERVES 4
Preparation: 5 minutes
Cooking: 15 minutes
Difficulty: ★
Cost: ★

UTENSILS

1 large sauté pan

◇ FRIED ONION RINGS ◇

Serve as a cocktail snack or as a garnish for grilled meats.

◇ Peel the onions and slice them into rings 2 mm (⅛ inch) thick. Soak the onion rings in the milk, then drain them and dip in the flour, to coat thoroughly. Shake off the excess flour.

◇ Heat oil in a deep-fryer to 190°C (375°F). Fry the onions briefly in the hot oil until golden. Drain on kitchen paper and serve immediately.

INGREDIENTS

150 g (5 oz) onions
250 ml (9 fl oz/1⅛ cups) milk
a little flour
oil for deep-frying

COCKTAIL SNACK OR GARNISH

SERVES 4
Preparation: 5 minutes
Cooking: 5 minutes
Difficulty: ★
Cost: ★

UTENSILS

1 bowl
1 deep-fryer
kitchen paper

◇ Peel the onions and cut away the top quarter of each. Bring a large saucepan of lightly salted water to the boil, add the onions and blanch for 5 minutes. Drain and refresh under cold running water to prevent further cooking. Drain well again.

◇ Meanwhile, wash the mushrooms and chop them finely. Chop the ham finely.

◇ Using a vegetable corer, hollow out the onions, leaving a shell 1 cm (½ inch) thick. Take care not to pierce the base or sides of the onions.

◇ Heat the oven to 180°C (350°F/Gas Mark 4).

◇ Chop the onion flesh from the centres. Melt the butter in a sauté pan and cook the chopped onion gently until transparent. Add the mushrooms, ham and sausagemeat. Season with salt and pepper. Mix well and cook gently until most of the mushroom liquid has evaporated.

◇ Fill the onions with the stuffing mixture and arrange them closely in a single layer in a buttered ovenproof dish. Pour in the wine and 50 ml (2 fl oz/¼ cup) water into the dish.

◇ Cover with foil and bake in the oven for 1½ hours, until the onions are tender when pierced with the point of a knife.

◇ Sprinkle the onions with breadcrumbs and brown under the grill for 5 minutes. Serve immediately.

INGREDIENTS

4 very large onions
salt
150 g (6 oz) mushrooms
100 g (4 oz) cooked ham
50 g (2 oz/4 tbsp) butter
150 g (6 oz) sausagemeat
pepper
50 ml (2 fl oz/¼ cup) dry white wine
dried breadcrumbs

FIRST COURSE

SERVES 4
Preparation: 10 minutes
Cooking: 1 hour and 40 minutes
Difficulty:*
Cost: *

UTENSILS

1 saucepan
1 ovenproof dish
kitchen foil
OVEN
180°C (350°F/Gas Mark 4)

•S H A L L O T S•

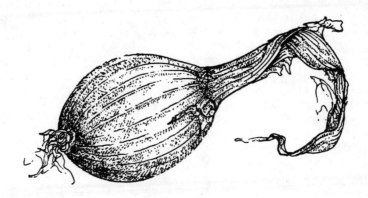

T HE SHALLOT IS one of the 450 members of the Allium family. It first grew
in the fertile soil of the Palestinian coastland 1200 years BC, and takes its
name from the city of Ascalon. The crusaders brought it back to Europe.

The shallot is more highly flavoured and digestible than the onion. It
contributes potassium, calcium and iron, Vitamin C and folic acid.

Shallots come in several colours and varieties. The grey–brown shallot is the
most common.

◇ BUYING SHALLOTS ◇

Look for good firm bulbs, with the skins intact and no sign of germination
taking place.

◇ PREPARING SHALLOTS ◇

Peel and cut away the small stumps of root and stalk.

◇ COOKING SHALLOTS ◇

Shallots are used to flavour an infinite variety of dishes rather than served as a
vegetable in their own right. Gently stewed in butter, they lose acidity and add
flavour to many sauces. They are used raw in vinaigrette.

Shallots can be used as a garnish if partially peeled and cooked in fat.

◇ CHEF'S TIPS ◇

Peeling shallots (and onions) becomes a much less painful exercise if they are
left for 10 minutes in the freezer, or for 1 hour in the refrigerator, before use.
They should then be peeled under a gently running cold tap.

The strong, lingering odour of shallots can be removed from the hands by
rubbing with coarse salt and rinsing under very cold water.

A warning: if shallots (and onions) are peeled and then only partly used,
they can become harmful if kept for any length of time.

◇ Trim the kidneys, leaving a thin layer of fat around them. Reserve the excess fat.

◇ Remove any loose papery skins from the shallots and trim away the roots, but do not peel them.

◇ In a small saucepan, melt the reserved veal kidney fat over a very gentle heat. Add the shallots and cook over a very gentle heat for 45 minutes; the fat should not bubble.

◇ Remove the cooked shallots with a slotted spoon and drain on kitchen paper. Squeeze the soft centres out of 10.

◇ Meanwhile, remove the membrane which surrounds the kidneys. Cut the kidneys in half lengthways. Remove all the central fat and core from the kidneys.

◇ Put a little of the kidney fat into a frying pan and fry the kidneys briskly for about 10 minutes, turning from time to time. Remove the kidneys from the pan and keep warm.

◇ Deglaze the pan with the wine, using a wooden spatula to scrape the base and sides, to loosen any sediment.

◇ Allow the sauce to reduce over a moderate heat for 2 minutes, then add the 10 shallot centres. Mix well, add the butter and season to taste with salt and pepper. Allow the sauce to simmer gently while you cut the cooked kidneys into slices about 2 mm ($\frac{1}{8}$ inch) thick.

◇ Pour a pool of the sauce on to each heated dinner plate. Arrange half a sliced kidney on each plate and garnish with 2 unpeeled cooked shallots.

INGREDIENTS

2 whole veal kidneys

18 shallots

100 ml (4 fl oz/$\frac{1}{2}$ cup) full-bodied red wine

20 g ($\frac{3}{4}$ oz/1$\frac{1}{2}$ tbsp) butter

salt and pepper

MAIN DISH

SERVES 4

Preparation: 45 minutes

Cooking: 10 minutes

Difficulty: ★★

Cost: ★★★

UTENSILS

1 small saucepan

1 frying pan

kitchen paper

1 wooden spatula

◇ SHALLOT RELISH ◇

Serve with charcuterie or potted meats.

◇ Peel the shallots and cut them into 2 mm ($\frac{1}{8}$ inch) slices. Melt the butter in a frying pan and cook the shallots gently until transparent. Do not allow them to brown.

◇ Add enough wine and vinegar in equal quantities to the pan to cover the shallots.

◇ Cook, uncovered, until all the liquid has evaporated and the shallots are of a jam-like consistency.

INGREDIENTS

300 g (10 oz) shallots

15 g ($\frac{1}{2}$ oz/1 tbsp) butter

about 300 ml (10 fl oz/$\frac{2}{3}$ cup) full-bodied red wine

about 300 ml (10 fl oz/$\frac{2}{3}$ cup) red wine vinegar

RELISH

SERVES 4

Preparation: 10 minutes

Cooking: 45 minutes

Difficulty: ★

Cost: ★

UTENSILS

1 frying pan

◇ First make the pastry. Combine the flour, butter and salt in a food processor or by hand until crumbly. Add the egg yolk and water and work until the dough holds together. Wrap in clingfilm and chill in the refrigerator for 1 hour.

◇ Heat the oven to 200°C (400°F/Gas Mark 6).

◇ Roll out the pastry and use to line a 20 cm (8 inch) flan tin. Prick the base and bake until the pastry is just cooked, but not browned (10–15 minutes).

◇ To prepare the filling, peel and trim the shallots. Melt 100 g (4 oz/6 tbsp) of the butter in a saucepan. Add the shallots and cook over a very low heat for about 45 minutes; the butter should not bubble.

◇ Remove the shallots with a slotted spoon and drain on kitchen paper for a few minutes. Reduce to a purée in a food processor or blender. Add the cream, egg yolks, salt and pepper. Whisk well.

◇ Soak sweetbreads in several changes of cold water for 2 hours. Cover with cold water add the lemon juice and simmer for 5 minutes. Plunge into cold water, gently pull away membrane, then pat dry.

◇ Cut the sweetbreads into 1 cm (½ inch) cubes. Fry them briskly in all but 15 g (½/1 tbsp) of the remaining butter in a frying pan until sealed and lightly coloured.

◇ Pour the vinegar into the pan. Use a wooden spatula to scrape the base and sides of the pan to loosen any sediment. Allow to cook for a few moments until the vinegar is reduced to a coating consistency. Add the sweetbreads and turn to coat.

◇ Tip the sweetbreads and sauce into the prepared pastry case. Spread the shallot purée on top. Bake in the oven for 15–20 minutes.

◇ Just before serving, melt the remaining butter and spoon it over the tart.

INGREDIENTS

FOR THE PASTRY

100 g (4 oz/⅞ cup) plain (all-purpose) flour

75 g (3 oz/5 tbsp) butter

a pinch of salt

1 egg yolk

15 ml (1 tbsp) cold water

FOR THE FILLING

200 g (7 oz) shallots

150 g (5 oz/1¼ sticks) butter

100 ml (4 fl oz/½ cup) double cream

2 egg yolks

salt and pepper

1 pair veal sweetbreads, weighing 200 g (7 oz)

juice of ¼ lemon

100 ml (4 fl oz/½ cup) red wine vinegar

FIRST COURSE

SERVES 4

Preparation: 55 minutes

Cooking: 35 minutes

Difficulty: ★★

Cost: ★★

UTENSILS

1 flan tin (tart pan/pie plate) 20 cm (8 inches) in diameter

1 food processor or blender

1 saucepan

1 frying pan

kitchen paper

1 wooden spatula

OVEN

200°C (400°F/Gas Mark 6)

◇ SHALLOT FRITTERS ◇

◇ To make the batter, pre-heat a mixing bowl by standing it in a larger bowl of boiling water.

◇ Put the yeast and salt into the bowl with 5 ml (1 tsp) warm water. When the yeast and salt are dissolved, add the oil and flour. Work the mixture well with your fingers. Cover and leave to stand for 2 hours in a warm place.

◇ Remove any loose papery skins from the shallots, and trim off the roots, but do not peel them. Melt the butter in a saucepan. Add the shallots and cook very gently for 45 minutes; the butter should not bubble.

◇ Remove the shallots with a slotted spoon and drain on kitchen paper. Peel the shallots.

◇ Heat oil in a deep-fryer to 190°C (375°F).

◇ When ready to use the batter, whisk the egg white stiffly and gently fold it into the batter mixture. Coat the shallots in the batter, then lower them into the hot oil and fry for a few seconds. Drain on kitchen paper and serve immediately.

INGREDIENTS

200 g (7 oz) shallots
150 g (5 oz/1¼ sticks) butter
oil for deep-frying
FOR THE BATTER
2.3 g (⅛ oz) fresh yeast or ⅜ tsp dried
a pinch of salt
10 ml (2 tsp) olive oil
*50 g (2 oz/6 tbsp) plain (all-purpose)
flour*
1 egg white

SIDE DISH

SERVES 4
Preparation: 10 minutes
2 hours standing time for the batter
Cooking: a few seconds
Difficulty: ★
Cost: ★

UTENSILS

1 mixing bowl
1 whisk
1 medium saucepan
1 deep-fryer
kitchen paper

◇ FRIED SHALLOT NIBBLES ◇

◇ Peel the shallots and slice them into 2 mm (⅛ inch) thick rounds.

◇ Heat oil in a deep-fryer to 190°C (375°F).

◇ Soak the shallot slices in the milk. Drain and dip in the flour, to coat thoroughly. Lower into the hot oil and fry for a few seconds, then drain on kitchen paper.

◇ Place the fried shallots slices on a heated serving dish and sprinkle lightly with salt and pepper.

INGREDIENTS

150 g (5 oz) shallots
oil for deep-frying
150 ml (5 fl oz/⅔ cup) milk
50 g (2 oz/6 tbsp) flour

COCKTAIL SNACK

SERVES 4
Preparation: 5 minutes
Cooking: 5 minutes
Difficulty: ★
Cost: ★

UTENSILS

1 deep-fryer
kitchen paper

·L E E K S·

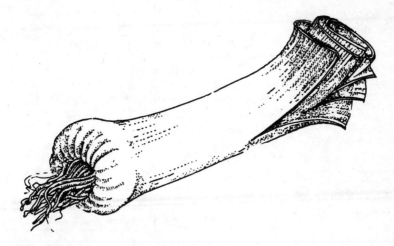

ANATOLE FRANCE CALLED the leek the poor man's asparagus, since with careful preparation it can stand comparison with any more sophisticated vegetable. And in addition to its flavour, the leek has many health-giving qualities; it is rich in Vitamin C, potassium, calcium, iron and fibre. It is also a diuretic, an antiseptic, an emollient and good for the lungs.

The origins of the leek are unknown, but we do know that the Egyptians ate it; indeed, the pharoah Cheops prized leeks so highly that he offered his soldiers leeks, rather than gold, as a reward. The Romans too prized leeks, and Nero was said to eat only leeks on certain days, to improve his voice. The Greeks prescribed leeks as a cure for sterility.

◇ BUYING LEEKS ◇

Buy the smallest leeks you can find. The green parts should be shiny and squeak when pressed. The white should be firm to the touch, with the roots still firmly attached. Allow 150–200 g (5–7 oz) per person.

◇ PREPARING LEEKS ◇

Cut away the roots level with the base. Remove any withered outer leaves and trim the top leaves, leaving about two-thirds of the leek intact. At the point where the white and green parts merge, slit upwards twice to cut the upper part of the leek into quarters. This will enable you to sluice out any soil or grit. Use the discarded leek leaves in soups and stocks.

Leeks are best served as an accompaniment to dishes that will not overwhelm their delicate flavour. They may be served in their own right, or used as a seasoning; if used to replace onions, they will give the dish a more delicate flavour.

If the leeks are large, cook them in boiling water for 8–10 minutes, tied in bundles of 4 or 5. After removing the bundles, untie them, so that the leeks can drain thoroughly. Then finish the cooking in butter, cream, etc.

If you are cooking small, young leeks, arrange them in a sauté pan with a little butter. Cover them with water and cook them gently, so that the water evaporates and the leeks glaze in the butter. Add a little more water if necessary.

When the leeks are being used as a seasoning, for example in a soup, slice them finely and sweat them in a little butter or oil. In this way, the leeks will lose much of their water content, and also any bitterness. They are ready for use when they are transparent. Do not allow them to brown.

◇ *LEEK TART* ◇

◇ First make the pastry. Combine the flour, butter and salt in a food processor or by hand until crumbly. Add the water and work until the dough holds together. Wrap in clingfilm and place in the refrigerator for 30 minutes.

◇ Heat the oven to 200°C (400°F/Gas Mark 6). Line a 20 cm (8 inch) flan tin with the pastry and bake until the pastry is just cooked, but not browned (10–15 minutes).

◇ Wash and trim the leeks as described on page 111. Slice them thinly and put them into a sauté pan with the butter. Sweat the leeks over a very gentle heat until they have exuded their water and become transparent. Do not let them brown. Add a little water to the leeks if necessary. When cooked, they should be tender and shiny. Allow the leeks to cool slightly.

◇ Mix the egg yolks with the cream and add to the cooked leeks. Pour this mixture into the pastry case and smooth the surface. Bake for 15–20 minutes, until the filling is set and lightly browned.

INGREDIENTS

FOR THE SHORTCRUST
PASTRY
*100 g (4 oz/⅔ cup) plain (all-purpose)
flour*
75 g (3 oz/5 tbsp) butter, diced
a pinch of salt
30 ml (2 tbsp) iced water
FOR THE FILLING
700 g (1½ lb) leeks
25 g (1 oz/2 tbsp) butter
2 egg yolks
30 ml (2 tbsp) double (heavy) cream

FIRST COURSE

SERVES 4–6
*Preparation: 50–60 minutes, including
resting time for pastry*
Cooking: 25–30 minutes
Difficulty: ★★
Cost: ★

UTENSILS

1 sauté pan
1 flan tin (tart pan/pie plate)
1 mixing bowl
1 rolling pin
1 small bowl
OVEN
200°C (400°F/Gas Mark 6)

◇ LEEKS IN VINAIGRETTE SAUCE ◇

A very simple first course, delicious if the leeks are cooked to perfection and the vinaigrette is tasty.

◇ Wash and trim the leeks as described on page 111. Bring a large saucepan of salted water to the boil, and add the leeks, tied in bundles, as described on page 112. Cook for just under 10 minutes, until the leeks are tender but not mushy.
◇ Remove the leeks and plunge them into cold water for 15 seconds, to prevent further cooking. Drain them and lay on a tea-towel to dry, then arrange in a serving dish.
◇ To make the vinaigrette, whisk all the ingredients together thoroughly. Pour it over the leeks while they are still tepid and serve immediately.

INGREDIENTS

700 g (1½ lb) tender, young leeks
salt
FOR THE VINAIGRETTE
75 ml (5 tbsp) groundnut (peanut) oil
30 ml (2 tbsp) sherry vinegar
30 ml (2 tbsp) red wine vinegar
1 shallot, peeled and finely chopped
a few chopped chives
a little chopped parsley
a little prepared mustard
pepper

FIRST COURSE

SERVES 4
Preparation: 5 minutes
Cooking: 10 minutes
Difficulty: ★
Cost: ★

UTENSILS

1 large saucepan
1 colander
1 small bowl

◇ LEEK AND POTATO SOUP ◇

◇ Scrub the potatoes, but do not peel them, then cut them into small pieces. To do this, first halve the potatoes lengthways, then cut each half lengthways into 3 pieces shaped like orange segments. Cut each piece crossways into pieces about 2 mm (⅛ inch) wide. Do not rinse the potato pieces; their starch will thicken the soup. Wash and trim the leeks as described on page 111. Slice them thickly. Melt the butter in a large saucepan and sweat the leeks gently until they begin to become transparent.
◇ Add the potatoes to the pan and pour in enough cold water to come three times as far up the pan. Add only a little salt. Bring to the boil, then cook briskly, uncovered, for 12 minutes.
◇ Remove the pan from the heat and stir in the cream. Check the seasoning and serve the soup immediately in heated soup plates.

INGREDIENTS

900 g (2 lb) potatoes
550 g (1¼ lb) leeks
40 g (1½ oz/3 tbsp) butter
salt
30 ml (2 tbsp) double (heavy) cream
pepper

FIRST COURSE

SERVES 4
Preparation: 15 minutes
Cooking: 20 minutes
Difficulty: ★
Cost: ★

UTENSILS

1 large saucepan

◇ MEDALLIONS OF MONKFISH WITH LEEKS AND RED PEPPER BUTTER ◇

Ask your fishmonger to slice the monkfish into medallions; there should be 3 or 4 per person.

◇ Core and seed the pepper. Cut it into thin strips. Wash and trim the leeks as described on page 111. Peel and finely chop the shallots.

◇ Heat the olive oil in a frying pan and cook the pepper strips very gently for 5 minutes. Reduce the pepper to a purée in a blender or food processor, then sieve to make a smooth purée. Set aside.

◇ Cut the leeks into 4–5 cm (1½–2 inch) lengths. Place in a sauté pan with 15 g (½ oz/1 tbsp) of the butter; add enough water just to cover and cook until the water has evaporated and the leeks are beginning to sizzle gently in the remaining juices. Keep warm.

◇ Fry the monkfish medallions in the remaining butter for 2–3 minutes on each side.

◇ Put the chopped shallot into a small saucepan with the wine. Boil until the liquid has almost entirely evaporated. Add the cream and allow it to reduce. Reduce the heat and whisk in the remaining butter, a little at a time. Add the pepper purée and mix well. Season to taste.

◇ Spoon a pool of the pepper butter sauce on to each heated dinner plate. Add 3–4 monkfish medallions to each plate, interspersed with pieces of leek.

INGREDIENTS

1 red sweet pepper
550 g (1¼ lb) tender, young leeks
2 shallots
10 ml (2 tsp) olive oil
100 g (4 oz/1 stick) butter, cut into small pieces
550 g (1¼ lb) monkfish, sliced into medallions
100 ml (4 fl oz/½ cup) dry white wine
salt and pepper

MAIN COURSE

SERVES 4
Preparation: 30 minutes
Cooking: 15 minutes
Difficulty: ★★
Cost: ★★

UTENSILS

1 large saucepan
1 frying pan
1 sauté pan
1 blender or food processor
1 small saucepan
1 balloon whisk

◇ GRATIN OF LEEKS ◇

In this dish boiled leeks are arranged on a bed of chopped tomato, topped with cream and browned in the oven.

◇ Skin and seed the tomatoes. Dice the flesh.

◇ Wash and trim the leeks as described on page 111. Peel and finely chop the shallot. Bring 2.8 litres (5 pints/3 quarts) water to the boil in a large saucepan and add a handful of coarse salt. Blanch the leeks in the boiling water for 8 minutes. Plunge them into iced water to prevent further cooking, then drain and lay on a tea-towel to dry. Cut the leeks into 4–5 cm (1½–2 inch) lengths.

◇ Melt the butter in a flameproof gratin dish and cook the shallot gently until transparent. Remove the dish from the heat and spread the diced tomato on top of the shallot. Arrange the leeks on top of them.

◇ Heat the oven to 200°C (400°F/Gas Mark 6).

◇ Place the cream in a small saucepan and boil gently until thick. Season the leeks with salt and pepper. Pour over the cream and bake for 15 minutes. Serve immediately.

INGREDIENTS

225 g (8 oz) tomatoes
1.4 kg (3 lb) leeks
salt
15 g (½oz/1 tbsp) butter
1 shallot
300 ml (10 fl oz/1¼ cups) double (heavy) cream
pepper

FIRST COURSE

SERVES 6
Preparation: 15 minutes
Cooking: 25–30 minutes
Difficulty: ★
Cost: ★

UTENSILS

1 large saucepan
1 flameproof gratin dish
1 small saucepan
OVEN
200°C (400°F/Gas Mark 6)

◇ LEEKS WITH SMOKED HADDOCK ◇

◇ Peel and very finely chop the shallot. Wash and trim the leeks as described on page 111, discarding all the green parts. Cook tied into bundles as described on page 112 in boiling water for just under 10 minutes, until tender but not mushy. Plunge the bundles into iced water, to prevent further cooking, then drain, untie the bundles and allow the leeks to cool completely. Then cut the leeks into 5 cm (2 inch) lengths.

◇ Mix the cream with the chopped shallot, lemon juice, pepper and a little salt. Pour a little shallot-flavoured cream on to each individual serving plate.

◇ Slice the smoked haddock as finely as possible, as though slicing smoked salmon. Wrap each piece of leek in a haddock slice and arrange on top of the cream.

INGREDIENTS

1 shallot
550 g (1¼ lb) leeks
200 ml (7 fl oz/⅞ cup) double (heavy) cream
juice of 1 lemon
4 slices smoked haddock fillet (see recipe)

FIRST COURSE

SERVES 4
Preparation: 15 minutes
Cooking: 10 minutes
Difficulty: ★
Cost: ★

UTENSILS

1 large saucepan
1 small bowl
1 sharp fish filleting knife

◇ Clean all the stock vegetables and cut them into small pieces. Place them in a large saucepan with the chicken carcass and/or giblets. Add the herbs, wine and water. Bring to the boil, then simmer for 30 minutes, skimming frequently. Strain.

◇ Meanwhile, peel and finely chop the shallot. Wash and trim the leeks as described on page 111 and chop them roughly. Put the leeks and shallots in a large saucepan with the butter and cook gently until they begin to become transparent. Add 450 ml (15 fl oz/2 cups) of the stock and the sausages and cover the pan. Simmer gently for 35 minutes. Serve in heated soup plates.

INGREDIENTS

1 shallot

1.1 kg (2½ lb) leeks

40 g (1½ oz/3 tbsp) butter

4 smoked sausages

FOR THE STOCK

50 g (2 oz) carrots

50 g (2 oz) mushrooms

1 small onion

1 small leek

1 celery stalk

1 garlic clove

450 g (1 lb) chicken carcass and/or giblets

1 thyme sprig

½ bay leaf

3 parsley stalks

100 ml (4 fl oz/½ cup) dry white wine

1.4 litres (2½ pints/1½ quarts) water

MAIN COURSE

SERVES 4

Preparation: 45 minutes

Cooking: 45 minutes

Difficulty: *

Cost: *

UTENSILS

2 large saucepans

1 fine sieve

·G A R L I C·

ORIGINATING IN ASIA, where large quantities of it are used, most notably in China, garlic has always traditionally had an important role to play in herbal medicine, religion and magic, as well as in the kitchen, in most countries. Even today, no other vegetable has so many attributed properties as garlic.

The Egyptians regarded garlic as sacred, and Cheops distributed daily rations of it to the labourers building the pyramids, to maintain their strength and help them ward off epidemics. Greek athletes and wrestlers would eat several cloves before entering into competition, to increase their strength. Roman patricians, judging garlic too plebeian for their own use, fed it to their fighting cocks; but the common people, peasants and military alike, would feast on this powerful tonic. In France, the monks grew great quantities of it in their gardens.

Popular mythology credits garlic with the power to keep vampires and evil spirits at bay; it also has an impressive (and better-documented) medicinal reputation. As a powerful disinfectant, it can be used to treat ulcers and unhealthy sores. It eases rheumatic pains, lowers blood cholesterol and therefore reduces certain cardiovascular problems, can be used as a remedy against coughs, pulmonary complaints, intestinal worms, whooping cough, hoarseness, loss of voice, etc. All this in addition to a number of vitamins and minerals, although it is usually eaten in very small quantities.

In the face of such powers, one might perhaps be tempted to eat garlic with every meal. But, as though to highlight its many virtues, garlic has one fault: it is an irritant to the stomach and the urinary tract, and should therefore be eaten in moderation.

◇ BUYING GARLIC ◇
Make sure that the cloves are firm and sound, particularly late in the season when they may have withered or begun to sprout.

117

◇ PREPARING GARLIC ◇

Peel each clove, unless the recipe specifies that the garlic should be cooked in its papery outer skin. By cutting the clove in half lengthways, you can remove the little green shoot which makes garlic hard to digest and which is responsible for the lingering aftertaste which many people find unpleasant.

◇ CHEF'S TIPS ◇

To get the fullest flavour from a peeled garlic clove, crush it with the flat of a knife-blade on a chopping board.

To flavour a salad, use oil infused with one or more peeled garlic cloves.

◇ KEBABS OF LANGOUSTINES WITH AIOLI AND BAKED POTATOES ◇

◇ Heat the oven to maximum temperature. Wash the potatoes, dry them well and halve them lengthways.

◇ Reduce the oven to 200°C (400°F/Gas Mark 6). Put the potatoes on a baking sheet, cut side uppermost. Sprinkle each one with a pinch of ground almonds. Bake in the oven for about 20 minutes, until tender. The potatoes will swell and turn golden-brown as they cook.

◇ Meanwhile, prepare the aioli sauce according to the instructions on page 121.

◇ Peel the langoustines and thread them on to kebab skewers. Brush them with olive oil. Heat the grill (broiler) to a high temperature and cook the langoustines briefly on each side, until cooked through.

◇ Serve the langoustines, potatoes and aioli sauce together.

INGREDIENTS

550 g (1¼ lb) small potatoes
15 ml (1 tbsp) ground almonds
8–12 langoustines (Pacific prawns are also suitable)
olive oil for brushing
FOR THE AIOLI
SAUCE
5 cloves garlic
200 ml (7 fl oz/⅞ cup) olive oil
1 small potato
1 egg yolk
10 ml (2 tsp) lemon juice
2.5 ml (½ tsp) mustard (optional)
salt and pepper

MAIN COURSE

SERVES 4
Preparation: 5–15 minutes
Cooking: 15–30 minutes
Difficulty: ★★
Cost: ★★

UTENSILS

4 kebab skewers
1 pestle and mortar
1 small balloon whisk
1 bowl
OVEN
maximum setting, then
200°C (400°F/Gas Mark 6)

◇ Clean the stock vegetables. Chop them coarsely. Put them into a saucepan with the herbs and 600 ml (1 pint/2½ cups) cold water. Bring to the boil, then simmer for 20–30 minutes. Strain off the liquid and discard the solids in the sieve.

◇ Season the chicken pieces with salt and pepper. Fry them in the olive oil in a sauté pan. When the chicken is nicely coloured on all sides, add the butter, garlic and bouquet garni. Cover the pan, reduce the heat and cook for further 12–15 minutes.

◇ Remove the chicken and garlic from the pan and keep warm. Discard the fat.

◇ Return the pan to the heat. Pour in 150 ml (5 fl oz/⅔ cup) of the vegetable stock. Scrape the base of the pan well, to loosen any sediment. Return the garlic to the pan and simmer gently for 10 minutes.

◇ Pass the sauce through a sieve, pressing the contents of the sieve well, so that the cooked garlic becomes a purée. Stir this into the sauce, to thicken it. Season to taste with salt and pepper and return to the pan. Return the chicken pieces to the pan, turn them in the sauce and reheat for 1 minute. Serve immediately.

INGREDIENTS

1 chicken weighing about 1.4 kg (3 lb), cut into 8 pieces

salt and pepper

10 ml (2 tsp) olive oil

75 g (3 oz/6 tbsp) butter

12 large garlic cloves, unpeeled

BOUQUET GARNI

a few parsley stalks

1 small thyme sprig

¼ bay leaf

1 small celery stalk

FOR THE VEGETABLE STOCK

1 onion

1 shallot

1 small leek

1 carrot

1 celery stalk

1 thyme sprig

1 bay leaf

1 parsley sprig

MAIN COURSE

SERVES 4

Preparation: 15–30 minutes

Cooking: 15–30 minutes

Difficulty: ★

Cost: ★

UTENSILS

1 saucepan

1 sauté pan with a lid

1 fine sieve

◇ Chop the lamb into even-sized pieces. Skin, seed and chop the tomatoes as described on page 27. Peel and finely chop the shallot.

◇ Heat the oil in a flameproof casserole and seal the pieces of lamb on all sides. When they are nicely browned, add the tomato, shallot, unpeeled garlic cloves, bouquet garni and the vegetable stock or water. Cover and simmer gently for 1½ hours.

◇ Meanwhile, heat the oven to 180°C (350°F/Gas Mark 4). Cut the green garlic in half horizontally. Put the pieces into an ovenproof dish and dot with butter. Add a few spoonfuls of the vegetable stock from the lamb to come halfway up the garlic. Bake in the oven for 15 minutes.

◇ When the lamb is tender, remove it from the liquid and keep warm. Pass the sauce through a sieve, pressing with the back of a spoon to extract as much flavour as possible from the vegetables. Season to taste with salt and pepper.

◇ Put the pieces of lamb on to a warmed serving dish. Coat with the sauce and surround with the baked garlic. Chop the basil finely and sprinkle it over the garlic just before serving.

INGREDIENTS

450 g (1 lb) breast of lamb
550 g (1¼ lb) neck of lamb
3 tomatoes
1 shallot
10 ml (2 tsp) groundnut (peanut) oil
12 garlic cloves, unpeeled
1 bouquet garni
750 ml (1¼ pints/3 cups) vegetable stock or water
2 bulbs green garlic (early growths, not ripe and dried)
15 g (½ oz/1 tbsp) butter
salt and pepper
1 basil leaf

MAIN COURSE

SERVES 4
Preparation: 5–15 minutes
Cooking: 1½ hours
Difficulty: ★
Cost: ★

UTENSILS

1 saucepan
1 flameproof casserole (preferably cast-iron)
1 small ovenproof dish
1 fine sieve
OVEN
180°C (350°F/Gas Mark 4)

◇ AIOLI SAUCE ◇

Aioli is a mayonnaise strongly flavoured with garlic. It is essential to use a good-quality olive oil, if possible virgin oil from a first cold pressing.

In Provence, it is customary to serve aioli with the following: boiled salt cod; snails cooked in water flavoured with fennel and onions studded with cloves; winkles or whelks; lightly boiled carrots, potatoes, globe artichokes, french beans and cauliflower; hard-boiled eggs. One may add to or omit from the list, according to personal taste.

◇ Peel and split the garlic cloves as described on page 118. Crush them in a mortar with 10 ml (2 tsp) of the oil until you have a smooth paste.
◇ Boil the potato, unpeeled, until cooked. Peel and while still hot, add it to the garlic paste. Pound until smooth.
◇ Put this mixture into a bowl. Add the egg yolk, half the lemon juice and the mustard, if you prefer a tangier mayonnaise. Mix these ingredients well, using a balloon whisk. Beat steadily until the yolk begins to turn pale. Then add the oil, drop by drop. (The idea that one must always beat in the same direction is false; the important factor is to maintain a regular, fairly slow rhythm.)
◇ When you have added about 30 ml (2 tbsp) of oil in this way, the mixture should resemble a thick paste. Then add the remaining lemon juice. The remaining oil can now be added in a steady trickle; you must continue to beat the mixture, but slightly faster than before. Season to taste with salt and pepper. Alternatively, make the aioli in a food processor.
◇ If the sauce becomes too thick, you may add a few drops of boiling water.

INGREDIENTS

5 garlic cloves
200 ml (7 fl oz/⅞ cup) olive oil
1 small potato
1 egg yolk
10 ml (2 tsp) lemon juice
2.5 ml (½ tsp) prepared mustard (optional)
salt and pepper

SAUCE

Preparation: 5–15 minutes
Cooking: 15–30 minutes
Difficulty: ★
Cost: ★

UTENSILS

1 pestle and mortar
1 balloon whisk
1 bowl

121

A good accompaniment for chicken, lamb or pork chops, or veal.

◇ Put the garlic into a saucepan of cold water and bring to the boil. Allow to boil for 2 minutes. Drain, then repeat the process twice more, to blanch the garlic. When you place the garlic in a fourth pan of water, the water should remain clear. Cook the garlic for about 10 minutes.

◇ Drain and peel the garlic. Purée the garlic in a blender or food processor.

◇ While the garlic is cooking, wash the mushrooms and cut off the stalks. Put the caps into a sauté pan, gills upwards. Dot with half the butter, sprinkle with half the lemon juice and cook over a gentle heat for 10 minutes. Cover the pan for the first 3 minutes, to allow the mushrooms to exude their liquid.

◇ Chop the mushroom stalks finely. Cook them in the same way as the caps, with the remaining butter and lemon juice, in an uncovered pan, to make a fairly dry purée.

◇ If the mushrooms are to be served with chicken, you may chop the chicken liver finely and add it to the stalks halfway through the cooking time.

◇ At the same time, bring the cream to the boil in a small saucepan and boil to reduce by about one-quarter. It should become smooth and fairly thick.

◇ Heat the oven to 180°C (350°F/Gas Mark 4).

◇ Mix together the mushroom purée, the parsley, the garlic purée and the reduced cream. If the mixture seems too liquid, return it to the heat for a few minutes, stirring constantly.

◇ Fill the mushroom caps with this mixture. Arrange them in an ovenproof dish and heat through in the oven for 5 minutes just before serving.

INGREDIENTS

10 garlic cloves, unpeeled
16 even-sized mushrooms, about 4 cm
(1½ inches) in diameter
15 g (½ oz/1 tbsp) butter
juice of ½ lemon
1 chicken liver (optional)
200 ml (7 fl oz/⅞ cup) double cream
5 ml (1 tsp) chopped parsley
salt and pepper

SIDE DISH

SERVES 4
Preparation: 5–15 minutes
Cooking: 5–15 minutes
Difficulty: ★
Cost: ★

UTENSILS

2 small saucepans
1 blender or food processor
2 sauté pans, 1 with a lid
1 ovenproof dish
OVEN
180°C (350°F/Gas Mark 4)

·ROOT· VEGETABLES AND TUBERS

◆ P O T A T O E S ◆

POTATOES CAME ORIGINALLY from Peru; they were brought back to Europe by the conquistadores. Although crops were then grown successfully in Holland and Ireland as well as Spain, other countries were slower to accept the potato. In France, for example, it was not until Antoine Parmentier won the support of Louis XVI and Marie Antoinette that potatoes became socially acceptable; his reward for this was to have his name attached to the French version of Shepherd's Pie ... Hachis Parmentier! The Dutch, the French and the British exported the potato to their colonies and it is now totally ubiquitous: you can even find deep-fried potatoes in Peking!

Contrary to popular belief, potatoes themselves do not actually put on weight; it is the method of preparation which may do the damage. Deep-fried potatoes can amount to as much as 253 calories per 100 g (4 oz). But provided the other ingredients used in their preparation are suitable, potatoes can be eaten by anyone ... even a baby as young as 5 months.

Freshly dug potatoes contain more Vitamin C than old potatoes. Potatoes also provide minerals, particularly potassium, together with protein, but no fats. The older a potato is, the more starch it contains. Potatoes also have valuable medical properties; those who suffer from ulcers are often told to eat mashed potato as part of their diet.

◇ BUYING POTATOES ◇

Look for firm potatoes with healthy skins and no obvious blemishes or signs of germination (remember, the skins are an important source of nutrients and can also be very tasty to eat). The variety of potato chosen will obviously depend on the recipe you have in mind, but in general you should use firm, waxy potatoes for frying, gratins, etc. and floury potatoes for mashing, use in soups, etc. Allow about 150–200 g (5–7 oz) per person – 250 g (9 oz) when making potato chips.

◇ PREPARING POTATOES ◇

Peel with care, removing any 'eyes' with a vegetable corer. Put the potatoes immediately into cold water, so that they do not discolour. But beware: if you leave the potatoes to soak for several hours, the outside will harden slightly, which will prolong cooking time.

In some recipes, such as Gratin Dauphinois, the potatoes should not be rinsed after being cut to the desired size, as the starch is needed to thicken the dish. But when making potato pancakes, for example, the potatoes should be thoroughly rinsed.

◇ COOKING AND SERVING POTATOES ◇

When boiling potatoes, always start them in cold water. Potatoes may also be steamed, baked, chipped, sautéed in butter or oil. In the case of sautéed potatoes, you have the option of par-boiling them first. Use a heavy frying pan which diffuses heat well, and start the cooking over a fairly high heat. Test if the potatoes are cooked by piercing with the point of a small sharp knife.

Potatoes go well with almost anything, particularly sauced and strongly flavoured dishes.

◇ BAKED BABY POTATO COCKTAIL SNACKS ◇

◇ Heat the oven to 200°C (400°F/Gas Mark 6).

◇ Wash the potatoes thoroughly and cut them in half lengthways; do not peel them.

◇ Place the potatoes, cut sides up, on a baking tray. Put a small pinch of ground almonds on each.

◇ Bake for about 15 minutes, until tender. The potatoes will swell and turn golden-brown. Add a light sprinkling of salt when they are ready. Serve hot.

INGREDIENTS

20 very small potatoes (Maris Piper or Pink Fir Apple)
20 g (¾ oz) ground almonds
salt

COCKTAIL SNACK

SERVES 4
Preparation: 5 minutes
Cooking: 10 minutes
Difficulty: ★
Cost: ★

UTENSILS

1 baking tray
OVEN
200° C (400°F/Gas Mark 6)

◇ POTATO PUREE ◇

Always use a wooden spoon or spatula to mash potatoes, not a whisk or food processor, which could make them rubbery.

◇ Peel and wash the potatoes. Cut them into quarters and put them into a saucepan of salted cold water. Boil the potatoes until tender.
◇ When the potatoes are cooked, drain them, place on a baking tray and dry in a hot oven for 5 minutes.
◇ Mash or rice the potatoes. Heat the milk and beat it in with the butter. Season to taste with salt and pepper. Serve the potato purée hot.

INGREDIENTS

450 g (1 lb) potatoes (Maris Piper)
salt
50 ml (2 fl oz/¼ cup) milk
75 g (3 oz/6 tbsp) butter
pepper

SIDE DISH

SERVES 4
Preparation: 5 minutes
Cooking: 15 minutes
Difficulty: *
Cost: *

UTENSILS

1 large saucepan
1 baking tray
1 potato masher or ricer
1 wooden spoon or spatula

◇ POTATOES WITH LEEK AND TRUFFLES ◇

◇ Slice the truffles thinly. Clean and slice the leek. Wash and peel the potatoes.
◇ Melt 20 g (¾ oz/1½ tbsp) of the butter in a sauté pan and sweat the leek gently, uncovered, until it exudes its liquid. Add the potatoes, the truffle juice and a little water (enough to half-cover the potatoes.) Season with salt and pepper. Cover and cook gently for 8–10 minutes, until the potatoes are tender.
◇ Remove the potatoes and keep warm. Boil the cooking juices until reduced by half. Whisk in the remaining butter and return the potatoes to the pan; add the truffles.
◇ Check the seasoning, add more pepper if necessary and serve immediately.

INGREDIENTS

100 g (4 oz) truffles
1 leek
400 g (14 oz) very small potatoes
(Maris Piper or Pink Fir Apple)
90 g (3½ oz/7 tbsp) butter
45 ml (3 tbsp) truffle juice

FIRST COURSE

SERVES 4
Preparation: 15 minutes
Cooking: 15 minutes
Difficulty: **
Cost: *****

UTENSILS

1 sauté pan
1 balloon whisk

◇ SAUTEED POTATOES ◇

If you use butter to fry the potatoes, the addition of a little oil will help to prevent the risk of burning.

◇ Peel the potatoes and cut them into rounds 2 mm (⅛ inch) thick. Wash and dry them thoroughly.
◇ Heat the oven to 240°C (475°F/Gas Mark 9).
◇ Heat the butter, with the oil, or fat. When it is very hot, add the potatoes, garlic and thyme. Fry, turning and stirring occasionally, until the potatoes are tender. Transfer the pan to the oven if the temperature seems to be dropping.
◇ When the potatoes are cooked, season them with salt and pepper and sprinkle with chopped parsley.

INGREDIENTS

800 g (1¾ lb) potatoes (Maris Piper or Pink Fir Apple)
3 garlic cloves, unpeeled
1 thyme sprig
75 g (3 oz/6 tbsp) butter, goose or duck fat
20 ml (4 tsp) oil
salt and pepper
1 small bunch of parsley

SIDE DISH

SERVES 4
Preparation: 5 minutes
Cooking: 10–15 minutes
Difficulty: ★★
Cost: ★

UTENSILS

1 large cast-iron frying pan
OVEN
240°C (475°F/Gas Mark 9)

◇ SAUTEED POTATOES AND CHESTNUTS ◇

A lovely dish for a cold winter's day, when you are serving casseroled game.

◇ Heat 45 ml (2 tbsp) of the oil in a frying pan and add the unpeeled chestnuts. Cook until lightly coloured through the shells, which will split and crack. One or two chestnuts may jump out of the pan, so watch it carefully.
◇ Drain the chestnuts, and when cool enough to handle, remove the outer shells and inner skins.
◇ Peel the potatoes and cut them into small chunks. Slice the celery thinly.
◇ Heat the remaining oil and half the butter in a frying pan and sauté the potatoes and celery. About 5 minutes before they are done, add the chestnuts and the remaining butter and fry until all the ingredients are tender. Pile into a heated serving dish and serve hot.

INGREDIENTS

75 ml (3 tbsp) groundnut (peanut) oil
400 g (14 oz) chestnuts, unpeeled
800 g (1¾ lb) potatoes (Maris Piper)
1 small celery stalk
50 g (2 oz/4 tbsp) butter

SIDE DISH

SERVES 4
Preparation: 15 minutes
Cooking: 15 minutes
Difficulty: ★
Cost: ★

UTENSILS

2 sauté pans

This tasty dish is similar to a Gratin Dauphinois in the manner of preparation, but the use of a light stock gives a more delicate end result. If possible, use home-made chicken stock; commercial stock cubes do not give as good a result.

◇ Clean and chop the stock vegetables. Put them into a large saucepan, together with the chicken carcass, broken up, the giblets, if used, the herbs, wine and 1.4 litres (2½ pints/1¼ quarts) cold water. Bring to the boil, then simmer for 35–40 minutes, skimming often. Strain.

◇ Trim, peel and slice the leeks and onions. Peel the potatoes, rinse them and cut into slices 2 mm (⅛ inch) thick. Do not rinse them again.

◇ Heat the oven to 180°C (350°F/Gas Mark 4).

◇ Put a gratin dish on the hob (burner) and melt the butter in it. Fry the leeks and onions gently until transparent. Add the potatoes and mix well. Season with salt and pepper.

◇ Add enough stock to come three-quarters of the way up the contents of the dish. Add the thyme, season with salt and pepper and bake for 1–1¾ hours, until lightly browned.

INGREDIENTS

100 g (4 oz) small leeks
100 g (4 oz) onions
1.1 kg (2¼ lb) potatoes
50 g (2 oz/4 tbsp) butter
a pinch of fresh thyme
salt and pepper
FOR THE CHICKEN STOCK
100 g (4 oz) carrots
50 g (2 oz) mushrooms
1 onion
1 celery stalk
1 leek
1 chicken carcass and giblets
1 garlic clove, crushed
1 thyme sprig
1 bay leaf
3 parsley stalks
200 ml (7 fl oz/⅞ cup) dry white wine

SIDE DISH

SERVES 4–6
Preparation: 45 minutes (including making the stock)
Cooking: 1–1¾ hours
Difficulty: ★
Cost: ★

UTENSILS

1 flameproof gratin dish
1 large saucepan
1 fine sieve
1 skimming ladle
OVEN
180°C (350°F/Gas Mark 4)

Long, slow cooking is the secret of a truly luscious Gratin Dauphinois; the potatoes should be completely impregnated with cream and milk.

◇ Peel the potatoes and cut them into slices 2 mm ($\frac{1}{8}$ inch) thick; do not rinse them after slicing.

◇ Peel 1 garlic clove and use to rub the inside of a large gratin dish. Grease the dish very generously with most of the butter and layer the potatoes in the dish. Season each layer with salt and pepper. Dot the top with the remaining butter.

◇ Heat the oven to 170°C (325°F/Gas Mark 3).

◇ Bring the cream to the boil and pour it over the potatoes. Mix well, so that the cream is evenly distributed through the potatoes. Then top up the dish with enough milk to cover the potatoes generously. Bury the 2 unpeeled garlic cloves in the potatoes, towards the top and middle of the dish.

◇ Cover with kitchen foil, set in a bain-marie and bake for about 3 hours, until the potatoes are tender.

◇ Just before serving, remove the foil, remove the garlic cloves and brown the potatoes under a hot grill (broiler).

INGREDIENTS

1.1 kg (2$\frac{1}{2}$ lb) potatoes
3 garlic cloves
50 g (2 oz/$\frac{1}{2}$ stick) butter
450 ml (15 fl oz/1$\frac{3}{4}$ cups) double (heavy) cream
about 300 ml ($\frac{1}{2}$ pint/1$\frac{1}{4}$ cups) milk
salt and pepper

SIDE DISH

SERVES 4–6
Preparation: 10 minutes
Cooking: 3 hours
Difficulty: ★
Cost: ★

UTENSILS

1 roasting pan or large shallow dish to use as bain-marie
1 large gratin dish
kitchen foil
OVEN
170°C (325°F/Gas Mark 3)

◇ FRENCH FRIED POTATOES ◇

Good French fries should be crisp outside and meltingly soft inside. To achieve this, they should be cooked in 2 stages. The first stage (called blanching, although it is done in oil, and not water) is to tenderize the chips. The second stage, done just before serving, is to make them crisp and golden.

◇ Peel the potatoes and cut them into strips of the required size; make sure that all are of similar size, so that they cook evenly. Wash and dry them thoroughly, so that the oil will not splutter when the potatoes are added.
◇ Heat oil in a deep-fryer to 190°C (375°F) and cook the potatoes for 7–8 minutes, until pale-coloured but tender. Drain them well and lay on kitchen paper. At this stage, the potatoes can be left for several hours if necessary before the second stage of cooking.
◇ Heat the oil to 180°C (350°F), add the potatoes and fry, shaking the basket from time to time, until nicely coloured. Remove and drain on kitchen paper.
◇ Pile the French fries on to a heated serving dish and sprinkle with salt.

INGREDIENTS

1.4 kg (3 lb) potatoes (Maris Piper or Pink Fir Apple) potatoes
groundnut (peanut) or grapeseed oil for deep-frying

SIDE DISH

SERVES 4–6
Preparation: 10 minutes
Cooking: 10 minutes
Difficulty: ★
Cost: ★

UTENSILS

1 deep-fryer
kitchen paper

◇ POTATO AND GRAPEFRUIT GRATIN ◇

This is a sort of tart without pastry, an attractively coloured potato dessert, to be served with a grapefruit salad.

◇ Heat the oven to 220°C (425°F/Gas Mark 7).
◇ Peel the potatoes and slice them as thinly as possible using a mandolin slicer or the finest slicing disc of a food processor; the slices should be almost transparent. Wash thoroughly under the cold tap, drain and dry very well.
◇ Put the potato slices into a mixing bowl and add the clarified butter and honey. Mix well to coat thoroughly.
◇ Arrange the potato slices on a baking tray in four circles, overlapping the slices slightly to form a rosette pattern. Bake for 10–12 minutes, until tender.
◇ Meanwhile, prepare the grapefruit. Cut thin slices from the top and the bottom of each grapefruit, then peel with a sharp knife, cutting away both skin and pith. Then divide the fruit into segments but do not try to remove the membrane between the individual segments.
◇ Place 2 grapefruit quarters on each individual serving plate and top with a 'cap' of baked potato slices. Serve immediately, to appreciate the hot/cold, soft/crunchy, sweet/sharp contrasts of this dish.

INGREDIENTS

200 g (7 oz) potatoes (Maris Piper)
100 g (4 oz/1 stick) butter, clarified
15 ml (1 tbsp) clear honey
2 grapefruit

DESSERT

SERVES 4
Preparation: 10 minutes
Cooking: 5–10 minutes
Difficulty: ★
Cost: ★

UTENSILS

1 small saucepan
1 mandolin slicer or food processor
1 mixing bowl
1 baking tray
OVEN
220°C (425°F/Gas Mark 7)

•JERUSALEM• ARTICHOKES

THE JERUSALEM ARTICHOKE is a small, pale tuber originating from Manchuria, where it was eaten only by princes. The taste of this small, twisted, knobbly root is midway between that of globe artichokes and salsify. In nineteenth-century Europe the Jerusalem artichoke was much prized; it then declined in popularity, but its use has increased in recent years.

◇ BUYING JERUSALEM ARTICHOKES ◇

Look for artichokes which are as fresh as possible; the pale, silvery skin should be so fine that there is no need for peeling. The tubers should be firm, with no signs of blemishes or darkening at the pointed ends. Use Jerusalem artichokes immediately. If stored, they will wilt and toughen.

Allow about 100 g (4 oz) per person.

◇ PREPARATION AND USE ◇

Although Jerusalem artichokes can be expensive, there is no waste, as the whole vegetable apart from the pointed tips can be used.

Cut away the pointed tips and wash the artichokes. If they are not absolutely fresh, peel them. Because of their tortuous shape, the easiest way to do this is to sprinkle coarse salt on to a dry tea-towel. Place the artichokes on top, fold the cloth over them and rub to remove the skins. Shake the artichokes into a colander and rinse in cold water.

◇ COOKING AND SERVING JERUSALEM ARTICHOKES ◇

Place the artichokes in a saucepan with enough cold water to cover, a nut of butter and a pinch of salt. Cook, uncovered, until the water has evaporated; very fresh artichokes will cook in about 5 minutes – 10 minutes is absolute maximum cooking time. When cooked, the artichokes should melt on the tongue and be velvety but not mushy.

You may also boil the artichokes in plain salted water and then sauté them in butter, but the first method retains their flavour and appearance better.

As Jerusalem artichokes have a naturally sweet flavour, be sparing in the use of salt and pepper.

Jerusalem artichokes are particularly good with fish, duck and venison. They will bring a touch of sweetness to any dish.

◇ COD FILLETS WITH JERUSALEM ARTICHOKES ◇

◇ Place the cod trimmings and bones in a saucepan with the onion and 3 parsley stalks. Cover with cold water. Bring to the boil, then simmer for 10 minutes. Strain through a fine sieve.

◇ Prepare the artichokes as described on page 131 and cook them in water and a little of the butter, as described above, then drain and keep warm.

◇ Heat the oven to 180°C (350°F/Gas Mark 4).

◇ Skin and seed the tomatoes; dice the flesh finely.

◇ Place several spoonfuls of the fish stock in an ovenproof dish. Arrange the cod fillets in the dish, cover with foil and bake in the oven for about 10 minutes.

◇ Boil the remaining fish stock to reduce to about 100 ml (4 fl oz/½ cup). Add the olive oil and return to the boil. Add the remaining butter, coriander seeds, lemon juice, diced tomato and salt and pepper. Mix well.

◇ Place 1 cod fillet on each heated dinner plate. Coat with sauce and sprinkle with chopped parsley. Surround with artichokes and serve.

INGREDIENTS

4 cod fillets, each weighing about 150 g
(5 oz), trimmings and bones reserved
½ onion, chopped
parsley
250 g (9 oz) Jerusalem artichokes
75 g (3 oz/6 tbsp) butter
2 ripe tomatoes
10 ml (2 tsp) olive oil
5 ml (1 tsp) coriander seeds
juice of ½ lemon
salt and pepper

MAIN COURSE

SERVES 4
Preparation: 10 minutes
Cooking: 10 minutes
Difficulty: ★★
Cost: ★

UTENSILS

2 large saucepans
1 sauté pan
1 ovenproof dish
1 fine sieve
1 small saucepan
kitchen foil
OVEN
180°C (350°F/Gas Mark 4)

Swiss chard is one of several leaf beets with thick white central stalks. The white and green parts of the leaves are cooked separately and may be served together or in separate dishes.

This dish may be served as a first course or side dish. As a first course, it will be enhanced if sprinkled with a little meat juice, from roast pork or chicken.

◇ Prepare a *beurre noisette* by melting 175 g (6 oz/1½ sticks) of the butter in a sauté pan, taking care that it does not burn. Keep it over a low heat and skim away the foam that forms, until the butter turns an attractive nut-brown. Remove from the heat and allow to cool.

◇ Prepare the artichokes as described on page 131. Cook them in water and half of the remaining firm butter as described on page 132.

◇ Cut the green leafy part of the chard away from the central ribs. Wash the leaves and ribs separately in plenty of cold water.

◇ Bring a saucepan of salted water to the boil. Cook the green leaves for 3–4 minutes. Plunge into cold water to prevent further cooking, then drain. Press out as much water as possible; rolling the leaves in a tea-towel may make this easier. Set aside.

◇ With a small knife, strip away the film that covers the chard ribs. Cut them crossways into 1 cm (½ inch) slices. Cook the slices for 5–10 minutes, until tender, in a blanching liquid of salted boiling water with the lemon juice and flour added. Drain and plunge into cold water to prevent further cooking. Drain well again, then sauté the slices in the remaining butter, adding a generous quantity of pepper.

◇ Meanwhile, fry the green leaves for 1 minute in the reheated *beurre noisette*.

◇ Put the green leaves into the base of a heated serving dish. Put the white ribs in the centre and arrange the artichokes around them.

INGREDIENTS

200 g (7 oz/1¾ sticks) butter
200 g (7 oz) artichokes
450 g (1 lb) Swiss chard
salt
juice of ½ lemon
10 ml (2 tsp) flour
pepper

HOT FIRST COURSE OR SIDE DISH

SERVES 4
Preparation: 20 minutes
Cooking: 10 minutes
Difficulty: ★
Cost: ★

UTENSILS

1 large saucepan
1 medium saucepan
1 sauté pan
1 sieve

◇ MEDALLIONS OF MONKFISH WITH JERUSALEM ARTICHOKES AND SWISS CHARD ◇

◇ Prepare and cook the artichokes and chard as described in Jerusalem Artichokes with Swiss Chard on page 133, setting aside 50 g (2 oz/4 tbsp) of the butter for frying the monkfish.

◇ Season the monkfish with salt and pepper. Fry in the reserved butter for 5 minutes.

◇ Arrange the monkfish medallions on top of the chard strips in the serving dish.

INGREDIENTS

200 g (7 oz) Jerusalem artichokes
450 g (1 lb) Swiss chard
250 g (9 oz/2¼ sticks) butter
salt and pepper
juice of ½ lemon
10 ml (2 tsp) flour
550 g (1¼ lb) monkfish, cut into small round slices 1 cm (½ inch) thick

MAIN COURSE

SERVES 4
Preparation: 20 minutes
Cooking: 20 minutes
*Difficulty: ***
*Cost: ****

UTENSILS

1 large saucepan
1 sauté pan
1 frying pan
1 sieve
1 medium saucepan

134

◇ ROAST CHICKEN WITH A GRATIN OF JERUSALEM ARTICHOKES ◇

◇ Heat the oven to 190°C (375°F/Gas Mark 5).

◇ Prepare the artichokes as described on page 131. Blanch them for 1 minute in boiling water, then drain.

◇ Meanwhile, spread the chicken with the butter and roast in a roasting pan or on a rotisserie attachment if you have one, for about 1 hour 20 minutes, until cooked through.

◇ 20 minutes before the chicken is cooked, pour its cooking juices into an ovenproof dish. Add the artichokes. Shake to coat with the juices and bake in the oven for 15 minutes.

◇ Serve the chicken accompanied by the artichokes, with any remaining cooking juices poured over.

INGREDIENTS

450 g (1 lb) artichokes
1 chicken weighing 1.4 kg (3 lb)
40 g (1½oz/3 tbsp) butter
salt and pepper

MAIN COURSE

SERVES 4
Preparation: 10 minutes
Cooking time: 1 hour 20 minutes
Difficulty: *
Cost: *

UTENSILS

1 roasting pan or rotisserie attachment
1 large saucepan
1 ovenproof dish
OVEN
190°C (400°F/Gas Mark 5) or rotisserie

◇ JERUSALEM ARTICHOKE FRITTERS ◇

◇ To make the batter, pre-heat a mixing bowl by standing it in a larger bowl of boiling water.

◇ Put the yeast, salt and 5 ml (1 tsp) warm water into the bowl. When the yeast and salt are dissolved, add the oil and flour. Work the mixture well with your fingers. Cover and leave to stand for 2 hours in a warm place.

◇ Prepare the artichokes as described on page 131. Cook them for 5–7 minutes only; they should remain slightly crisp. Plunge the artichokes into cold water to prevent further cooking. Drain them immediately and lay them on a tea-towel to dry.

◇ Heat oil in a deep-fryer to 190°C (375°F).

◇ When ready to use the batter, whisk the egg white stiffly and gently fold into the batter mixture. Dip the artichokes into the batter. Lower them into the hot oil and fry until golden-brown, then drain on kitchen paper to remove as much oil as possible. Sprinkle the fritters with salt and serve immediately.

INGREDIENTS

450 g (1 lb) Jerusalem artichokes
FOR THE BATTER
2–3 g (⅛oz) fresh yeast or ⅜ tsp dried
a pinch of salt
10 ml (2 tsp) oil
50 g (2 oz/6 tbsp) plain (all-purpose) flour
1 egg white

SIDE DISH

SERVES 4
Preparation: 10 minutes
2 hours resting time
Cooking: 10 minutes
Difficulty: *
Cost: *

UTENSILS

1 large saucepan
1 deep-fryer

◇ Prepare and cook the artichokes and chard as described in Jerusalem Artichokes with Swiss Chard on page 133, setting aside 50 g (2 oz/4 tbsp) of the butter for frying the chicken.

◇ Fry the chicken in the reserved butter in a flameproof casserole until nicely browned on all sides, adding the garlic cloves after a few minutes. Reduce the heat and cook, uncovered, for a further 10–15 minutes, turning often and ensuring that the butter does not burn, until the chicken is cooked through.

◇ Remove the chicken from the casserole and keep warm. Spoon off and discard about half the fat, leaving the garlic in the casserole.

◇ Deglaze the casserole with the chicken stock, scraping the base and sides well, to loosen any sediment. Boil briskly to reduce by two-thirds. Season with salt and pepper and mix well.

◇ Return the artichokes, chard rib slices and chicken to the casserole.

◇ Arrange the green chard leaves in a heated serving dish. Arrange the chicken, artichokes and chard rib slices on top. Coat with the remaining cooking juices from the casserole.

INGREDIENTS

450 g (1 lb) Jerusalem artichokes
450 g (1 lb) Swiss chard
250 g (9 oz/2¼ sticks) butter
salt and pepper
juice of ½ lemon
10 ml (2 tsp) flour
*1 chicken weighing 1.4 kg (3 lb), cut
into 8 pieces*
6 garlic cloves, unpeeled
250 ml (9 fl oz/1¼ cups) chicken stock

MAIN COURSE

SERVES 4
Preparation: 20 minutes
Cooking: 50–60 minutes
Difficulty: ★
Cost: ★

UTENSILS

1 flameproof casserole
1 frying pan
1 large saucepan
1 fine sieve
1 medium saucepan

•C A R R O T S•

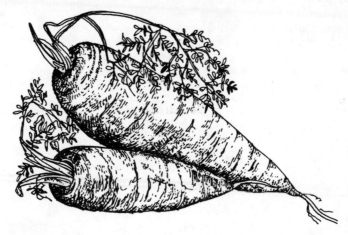

ALTHOUGH ORIGINALLY NATIVES of Afghanistan and the surrounding regions, carrots were grown more than 2,000 years ago in the Mediterranean area.

The Italians introduced the carrot to France during the Renaissance; in England at the court of Charles I, fashionable women wore carrot foliage as an ornament. The carrot did not attain general popularity until the eighteenth century, but it is now a highly popular vegetable to which many qualities are attributed. A diet including carrots will give protection against many health problems: its high carotene (Vitamin A) content protects against night blindness, and mucous membranes against infection. Its folic acid protects against anaemia and other health problems. The Vitamin C it contains has many roles in the body – including promoting healthy skin and reducing cold symptoms. Carrots also supply plenty of potassium and valuable amounts of calcium.

◇ BUYING CARROTS ◇

Remember that the brighter orange a carrot is, the more sweet and tender it will be. The skin should be smooth and unblemished; the tops should still be firmly attached.

Carrots sold in plastic packaging often 'sweat'. The resultant moisture can cause mould to form, so it is wiser to buy carrots loose. Allow 3–4 small carrots per person as a garnish, 100–150 g (4–5 oz) as a vegetable accompaniment.

◇ PREPARING THE CARROTS ◇

Scrape or brush carrots. The skin is rich in vitamins, so avoid peeling them if possible.

If the carrots are large, cut them lengthways into halves or quarters. Remove the central core. Do not make the mistake of attempting to trim carrots down, so that you are left with only the central part!

◇ COOKING AND SERVING CARROTS ◇

Carrots should always be cooked in water and butter. Blanch them for a few minutes in boiling water. Then put them into a sauté pan with a lid, together with some butter and a pinch of sugar. Add enough water to just cover the carrots. Simmer them gently. The water will evaporate, leaving the carrots in a little syrupy juice. Cook for 8–15 minutes, depending on size and age.

Serve the carrots with anything that will blend happily with their natural sweetness. As well as providing vegetable side dishes, carrots can be used in soups and raw salads, or they can be juiced to provide a drink.

◇ BABY CARROTS IN CREAM ◇

◇ Scrape the carrots. Cut them into very thin rounds not more than 2 mm (⅛ inch) thick, preferably using a mandolin slicer or food processor.

◇ Melt a little of the butter in a large frying pan with a lid. Add the carrots, cover and cook gently for a few minutes, until they exude their juice.

◇ When the carrots begin to soften, add the cream to the pan, raise the heat and allow it to reduce.

◇ When the carrots are cooked, add salt, pepper and lemon juice. Sprinkle with parsley just before serving.

INGREDIENTS

800 g (1¾ lb) baby carrots
50 g (2 oz/4 tbsp) butter
200 ml (7 fl oz/⅞ cup) double (heavy) cream
salt and pepper
juice of ½ lemon
a little chopped parsley

SIDE DISH

SERVES 4–6
Preparation: 5 minutes
Cooking: 5–15 minutes
Difficulty: ★
Cost: ★

UTENSILS

1 mandolin slicer or food processor
1 large frying pan with a lid

◇ WHIPPED CARROT PUREE ◇

◇ Scrape the carrots. Wash them and boil until tender.

◇ While the carrots are cooking, bring the cream to the boil in a small saucepan and allow it to reduce.

◇ Drain the cooked carrots and reduce them to a purée in a food mill, blender or food processor, then sieve to make a smooth purée.

◇ Heat the butter gently in a frying pan. Allow it to turn nut-brown, then add the carrot purée and mix well. Add the reduced cream and salt and pepper to taste. Whisk well to blend thoroughly.

INGREDIENTS

900 g (2 lb) carrots
300 ml (10 fl oz/1¼ cups) double (heavy) cream
75 g (3 oz/6 tbsp) butter
salt and pepper

SIDE DISH

SERVES 8
Preparation: 5 minutes
Cooking: 15–20 minutes
Difficulty: ★
Cost: ★

UTENSILS

1 large saucepan
1 small saucepan
1 food mill, blender or food processor
1 sieve
1 frying pan
1 balloon whisk

◇ CALF'S LIVER WITH VINEGAR AND CARROTS ◇

◇ Scrape and wash the carrots. Cut them into julienne strips 1 mm ($\frac{1}{16}$ inch) thick and about 5 cm (2 inches) long.

◇ Melt 15 g (½ oz/1 tbsp) of the butter in a frying pan with a lid. Add the carrot strips and 20 ml (4 tsp) water. Cover and cook over a low heat for 5 minutes.

◇ Melt the remaining butter in another frying pan. Fry the liver quickly on each side; it should be slightly pink in the middle. Remove the liver from the pan and keep hot.

◇ Deglaze the pan with the vinegar, scraping the base and sides well, to loosen any sediment. Allow the liquid to reduce until syrupy.

◇ Arrange the liver on a heated serving dish. Coat it with the sauce and surround with the julienne of carrots. Season with salt and pepper just before serving.

INGREDIENTS

4 carrots
50 g (2 oz/4 tbsp) butter
4 slices of calf's liver, each weighing 100 g (4 oz)
100 ml (4 fl oz/½ cup) vinegar, preferably raspberry
salt and pepper

MAIN COURSE

SERVES 4
Preparation: 5–10 minutes
Cooking: 10 minutes
Difficulty: ★
Cost: ★★

UTENSILS

2 frying pans, 1 with a lid
1 wooden spatula

◇ Bring a large saucepan of well-salted water to the boil. Add the vinegar and drop in the crab. Return to the boil, then cook for 8 minutes. Drain the crab and allow to cool.

◇ While the crab is cooling, wash and trim the leeks. Bring a saucepan of lightly salted water to the boil and cook the leeks for 8–10 minutes. Transfer them to a bowl of cold water, to prevent further cooking and preserve the colour. Drain well.

◇ Lay the crab on its back. Twist off the claws and crack them open to remove the meat. Set this aside.

◇ Remove the pointed flap from the crab's body. Separate the upper and lower shells. Discard the 'dead men's fingers', the spongy strips which are in fact the crab's gills.

◇ Press down on the small mouth part; it will snap away. When you lift it out, the crab's stomach will also come away.

◇ Use a skewer to remove the shreds of white meat from the main part of the body; it is divided into small sections, so this is a slow process. Set aside.

◇ Crush the crab shells in a mortar with a pestle (a solid bowl and a rolling pin make reasonable substitutes). Put the crushed shells and the yellow-brown body meat into a saucepan with the cream. Cook over a gentle heat for 15 minutes, until cream is reduced and thickened.

◇ While the cream is reducing, scrape and wash the carrots. Cut them into small pieces. Put them in a saucepan, add enough cold water to cover and boil until tender. Drain the carrots and reduce them to a purée in a food mill, blender or food processor, then sieve to make a smooth purée.

◇ Put the crab-shell cream through a very fine sieve, return it to a clean saucepan and continue to reduce it until it is very smooth and thick.

◇ Add 50 g (2 oz/4 tbsp) of the butter and whisk vigorously to emulsify the mixture. Add the carrot purée, season to taste with salt and pepper and mix well.

◇ Put a layer of carrot butter on each individual serving plate. Divide the white crabmeat among the plates.

◇ Fry the leeks in the remaining butter for 2 minutes, to reheat them. Arrange them around the edge of the plates.

INGREDIENTS

salt

100 ml (4 fl oz/½ cup) malt vinegar

1 large crab

200 g (7 oz) small leeks

300 ml (10 fl oz/1¼ cups) double (heavy) cream

200 g (7 oz) carrots

65 g (2½ oz/5 tbsp) butter, slightly softened

FIRST COURSE

SERVES 4

Preparation: 5–15 minutes

Cooking: 15–30 minutes

Difficulty: ★★

Cost: ★★

UTENSILS

1 large saucepan

1 pestle and mortar

2 medium saucepans

1 food mill, blender or food processor

1 fine sieve

1 balloon whisk

1 frying pan

·T U R N I P S·

THE ORIGINS OF the turnip are unknown, but we do know that it formed part of the diet of prehistoric man, and in medieval Europe was the basis of the ordinary person's diet, along with the cabbage.

In the days when vegetables were not treated with chemical fertilizers or insecticides, the turnip was much used for medicinal purposes. It was known to be a diuretic and a remedy for stomach ache. Moreover, as an extraction, it was used to treat asthma and lingering coughs; as a poultice, it was effective against skin irritations, chilblains and gout. In addition to all these virtues and the many excellent recipes in which it appears, the turnip has yet another claim to recognition. Sir Thomas Elyot, an English scholar and diplomat of the sixteenth century, wrote that it 'augmented Man's power of seduction and stimulated his carnal appetites'.

Turnips, despite a high water content, still contribute valuable amounts of Vitamin C, potassium and calcium.

◇ BUYING TURNIPS ◇
Look for pale, firm, unspotted roots. If the flesh is not close-grained, the turnip is not of good quality.

◇ PREPARING TURNIPS ◇
Use an ordinary kitchen knife, and not a vegetable peeler, when preparing turnips. This will enable you to remove the outer skin and the layer immediately beneath it. Hollow out the area immediately beneath the stalk.

◇ COOKING AND SERVING TURNIPS ◇
Turnips can either form part of a soup or stew, or they may be blanched, finished in butter and served as an accompaniment. To blanch, place the turnips in a saucepan of cold water and bring it to the boil, then drain.

Turnips are particularly good with rabbit and duck.

◇ TURNIPS WITH BACON ◇

◇ Peel and wash the turnips. Cut them into slices 2 mm (⅛ inch) thick, ideally using a mandolin cutter or food processor.

◇ Cut the bacon into matchstick lengths. Put them into a saucepan of cold water, bring to the boil, then immediately remove from the heat. Drain, rinse the lardons in cold water and dry them on kitchen paper.

◇ Heat the oil in a large sauté pan and fry the lardons until crisp and well-browned.

◇ Add the turnips to the pan. Stir well so that they are all coated with fat. Cook, stirring frequently, until the turnips are tender. Season with a little salt and plenty of pepper. Serve immediately.

INGREDIENTS

800 g (1¾ lb) turnips
200 g (7 oz) streaky bacon in 1 piece
30 ml (2 tbsp) groundnut (peanut) oil

FIRST COURSE OR SIDE DISH

SERVES 4
Preparation: 5–15 minutes
Cooking: 15–30 minutes
Difficulty: *
Cost: *

UTENSILS

1 large sauté pan
1 mandolin cutter or food processor
1 small saucepan
1 colander
kitchen paper

◇ BABY TURNIPS STUFFED WITH MUSHROOMS ◇

◇ Heat the oven to 200°C (400°F/Gas Mark 6).

◇ Peel the turnips, leaving the stems intact, and place in a saucepan of cold water. Bring to the boil and blanch for 3 minutes, then drain.

◇ Place the turnips in a buttered ovenproof dish. Add water until the turnips are almost, but not totally, covered. Sprinkle with salt. Cover with foil and bake in the oven for 1½ hours, until tender when pierced.

◇ Meanwhile, wash and dry the mushrooms, and chop finely. Peel and finely chop the shallot. Melt the butter in a saucepan, add the shallot and cook gently until transparent. Add the chopped mushrooms, salt and pepper. Mix thoroughly and cook gently, stirring frequently, until almost all the liquid has evaporated.

◇ Bring the cream to the boil in a small pan. Boil until slightly reduced and thickened. Skin, seed and slice the tomatoes (see page 27).

◇ Remove the cooked turnips from the oven. Drain them and cut each in half. Fill with the mushroom mixture.

◇ Replace the tops.

◇ Pour a pool of the hot cream on to each heated individual serving plate and divide the turnips among the plates. Garnish with tomato slices and chervil sprigs.

INGREDIENTS

800 g (1¾ lb) small turnips, with green tops
200 g (7 oz) mushrooms
½ shallot
25 g (1 oz/2 tbsp) butter
225 ml (8 fl oz/1 cup) double (heavy) cream
2 large tomatoes
chervil sprigs

FIRST COURSE

SERVES 4
Preparation: 5–15 minutes
Cooking: 1½ hours
Difficulty: *
Cost: *

UTENSILS

2 saucepans
1 ovenproof dish
1 vegetable corer
OVEN
200°C (400°F/Gas Mark 6)

◇ TURNIP SOUP ◇

◇ Chop the chicken carcass. Place it in a large saucepan with 2.6 litres (4½ pints/2½ quarts) water. Add 1 onion, cleaned and chopped, and the bouquet garni. Bring to the boil. Skim, then simmer gently for 25 minutes. Pour off the liquid and leave it to stand for a few minutes, then skim off the surface grease or blot with kitchen paper.

◇ Peel and chop the turnips, and peel, trim and chop the remaining onion and the leek. Melt the butter in a large saucepan. Add the onion and leek and cook gently until transparent. Add the turnips and cook gently for 4–5 minutes: do not allow to brown. Then add 2.3 litres (4 pints/2 quarts) of the chicken stock. Season lightly with salt and pepper.

◇ Bring to the boil, then simmer for 45 minutes, until the vegetables can be broken up easily with a fork.

◇ Reduce the contents of the pan to a purée in a blender or food processor. Add the cream and check the seasoning. Whisk to blend. Pour into a heated tureen and sprinkle generously with chervil.

INGREDIENTS

1 cooked chicken carcass
2 onions
1 bouquet garni
700 g (1½ lb) turnips
½ leek
50 g (2 oz/4 tbsp) butter
salt and pepper
150 ml (5 fl oz/⅔ cup) double (heavy) cream
chopped chervil

FIRST COURSE

SERVES 4
Preparation: 15–30 minutes
Cooking: 45 minutes
Difficulty: ★
Cost: ★

UTENSILS

2 large saucepans
1 blender or food processor
1 balloon whisk
1 fine sieve
1 skimmer
kitchen paper

◇ BRAISED DUCK WITH TURNIPS ◇

◇ Peel the turnips and potatoes. Cut them into quarters.

◇ Divide each duck portion in half, across the joint. Heat the oil in a flameproof casserole and fry the duck pieces briskly for about 10 minutes, until well-coloured.

◇ Add the turnips, potatoes and bouquet garni to the casserole. Season with salt and pepper. Add enough water to come two-thirds of the way up the contents of the casserole. Cover and bring to the boil, then simmer gently for 20 minutes.

◇ Discard the bouquet garni; check the seasoning and serve immediately.

INGREDIENTS

450 g (1 lb) turnips
450 g (1 lb) potatoes
4 duck leg portions
30 ml (2 tbsp) groundnut (peanut) oil
1 bouquet garni

MAIN COURSE

SERVES 4
Preparation: 5–15 minutes
Cooking: 40 minutes
Difficulty: ★
Cost: ★

UTENSILS

1 large flameproof casserole

·BEETROOT·

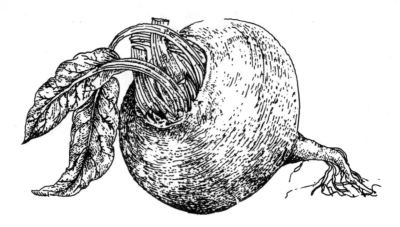

Beetroot originated in North Africa. The Greeks and the Romans grew it, but for the leaves rather than the roots. Pliny claimed that the leaves had the power to restore wine that had deteriorated in storage to its original taste; the famous Roman gastronome Apicius recommended them as a cure for constipation.

Beetroot became known in France during the Renaissance. Napoleon encouraged the planting of sugarbeet and also advocated the use of a beet which had been recently bred by a German: the red-fleshed beet, which was the beetroot as we know it.

Beetroots contribute potassium, calcium in particular, together with a little Vitamin C and folic acid. Though we are generally used to eating it cold in salads, it can also be delicious served hot.

◇ BUYING BEETROOT ◇

Much of the beetroot which is available commercially is pre-cooked. If possible, buy beetroot that has been baked, since this preserves flavour and nutritional value better than boiling. Baked beetroot can be recognized by its wrinkled, near-black skin. Boiled beetroot looks more attractive, but has less flavour. Look for small beets; larger ones are often fibrous. The older a root is, the more indigestible it becomes.

◇ CHEF'S TIP ◇

Use lemon juice to remove any beetroot juice stains from your fingers.

◇ MOULES MARINIERE WITH BEETROOT ◇

◇ Wash and brush the mussels well under cold running water. Pull off any loose beards. Put the mussels into a large saucepan and add the wine. Cover and set over a high heat until the mussels have opened. Discard any that have not opened.

◇ Remove the mussels from the pan. Shell them and set the flesh aside. Reserve the cooking liquid and any liquid in the shells.

◇ Peel the beetroot. Cut it into matchsticks about 5 cm (2 inches) long and 2 mm ($\frac{1}{8}$ inch) thick. Put these matchsticks into a frying pan with the butter and cook over a low heat for a few minutes, to allow the beetroot to exude its liquid.

◇ Pass the mussel cooking liquid through a sieve lined with muslin (cheesecloth), to remove any sand or grit from the mussels. Then return the liquid to the saucepan with the cream, the lemon juice and a generous sprinkling of pepper. Bring to the boil, then boil to reduce, until slightly thickened.

◇ Return the mussels to the pan and reheat gently. On no account allow them to boil.

◇ Immediately ladle the soup into heated soup bowls and garnish with the beetroot matchsticks.

INGREDIENTS

2.3 litres (3 pints) live mussels
100 ml (3 fl oz) dry white wine
100 g (4 oz) raw beetroot
15 g ($\frac{1}{2}$ oz/1 tbsp) butter
150 ml (5 fl oz/$\frac{2}{3}$ cup) double (heavy) cream
juice of 1 lemon
pepper

FIRST COURSE

SERVES 4
Preparation: 15 minutes
Cooking: 10 minutes
Difficulty: *
Cost: *

UTENSILS

1 large saucepan
1 sieve
1 frying pan

◇ FRIED WHITING WITH BEETROOT BUTTER ◇

◇ Cut the beetroot into 2 mm ($\frac{1}{8}$ inch) dice.

◇ Soften 100 g (4 oz/1 stick) of the butter. Add 20 ml (4 tsp) of the diced beetroot, with salt, pepper and the lemon juice. Mix together thoroughly, so that the beetroot is evenly distributed throughout the butter.

◇ Form the butter into a cylinder about 3 cm (1$\frac{1}{4}$ inches) in diameter. Wrap it in foil and refrigerate for at least 1 hour, until very firm.

◇ Melt the remaining butter in a frying pan. Fry the whiting fillets for 2–3 minutes and then arrange them in a heated flameproof serving dish.

◇ Cut the chilled beetroot butter into slices about 2 mm ($\frac{1}{8}$ inch) thick. Put 1 or 2 slices on each whiting fillet and flash the dish under the grill (broiler) for a few seconds. The butter should begin to melt, but still be creamy. Serve immediately.

INGREDIENTS

$\frac{1}{2}$ cooked beetroot
125 g (5 oz/1$\frac{1}{4}$ sticks) butter
salt and pepper
juice of 1 lemon
4 whiting fillets

MAIN COURSE

SERVES 4
Preparation: 15 minutes plus 1 hour
Cooking: 10 minutes
Difficulty: **
Cost: **

UTENSILS

1 frying pan
kitchen foil
1 flameproof serving dish

◇ SADDLE OF HARE IN BITTER SWEET SAUCE, WITH BEETROOT PUREE ◇

◇ First make the beetroot purée. Peel and thinly slice the onion. Melt 15 g ($\frac{1}{2}$ oz/1 tbsp) of the butter over a low heat and cook the onion very gently until transparent.

◇ Peel the beetroot and chop it into pieces the size of a small walnut. Add this to the onion, together with 30 ml (2 tbsp) each of wine and sherry vinegar. Cover and cook very gently for 20 minutes. Add salt and pepper and 15 g ($\frac{1}{2}$ oz/1 tbsp) of the butter and blend to a purée in a blender or food processor. Keep hot.

◇ Heat the oven to 230°C (450°F/Gas Mark 8).

◇ Remove the membrane from the surface of the hare. Put it to one side with any other trimmings. Season the hare with salt and pepper, melt 15 g ($\frac{1}{2}$ oz/1 tbsp) butter in a roasting pan and brown the hare on all sides. Add any reserved hare trimmings to the pan, to enhance the flavour of the sauce.

◇ When the meat is nicely browned, put it into the oven and cook for 12–15 minutes. The meat should be pink inside.

◇ Remove the pan from the oven. Remove the hare and keep it warm, wrapped in foil. Put the pan over a high heat, add the remaining vinegars and 50 ml (2 fl oz/$\frac{1}{4}$ cup) water. Deglaze the pan, scraping the base and sides well to loosen any sediment. Boil the liquid to reduce, until syrupy. Add the remaining butter and salt and pepper to taste. Remove from the heat and sieve the sauce.

◇ Carve the hare and arrange the slices on heated dinner plates. Coat the meat with the sauce and add 1 or 2 spoonfuls of beetroot purée.

INGREDIENTS

1 onion
50 g (2 oz/4 tbsp) butter
200 g (7 oz) cooked beetroot
50 ml (2 fl oz/$\frac{1}{4}$ cup) red wine vinegar
50 ml (2 fl oz/$\frac{1}{4}$ cup) sherry vinegar
salt and pepper
1 saddle of hare

MAIN COURSE

SERVES 4
Preparation: 10 minutes
Cooking: 35 minutes
Difficulty: ★★
Cost: ★★★

UTENSILS

1 saucepan
1 roasting pan
1 blender or food processor
1 sieve
OVEN
230°C (450°F/Gas Mark 8)

•CELERIAC•

Celeriac is just as full of flavour as its cousin the green or white 'branch' celery.

◇ BUYING CELERIAC ◇

Choose a root that weighs heavy in the hand and is unblemished. Do not be put off by the lumpy appearance of the root.

◇ PREPARING CELERIAC ◇

Use the trimmed and peeled white flesh. Cut away the leaves and any small roots. Peel fairly thickly, using a sharp knife. As celeriac discolours quickly once cut, put it into a bowl of acidulated water as you work.

◇ COOKING AND SERVING CELERIAC ◇

Cut the prepared roots into quarters, or slices 1 cm ($\frac{1}{2}$ inch) thick, depending on their size.

Bring a saucepan of water to the boil; add a squeeze of lemon juice. Cook the celeriac for 10–15 minutes. Drain, and finish the cooking in butter, meat juices, etc.

Serve celeriac with roast and casseroled meats. It is especially good with venison and game birds.

◇ CELERIAC REMOULADE ◇

Make sure that the ingredients and utensils for the mayonnaise are at room temperature. Remove the eggs from the refrigerator 2 hours before use.

◇ Make the mayonnaise, adding the mustard with the vinegar.
◇ Peel the celeriac as described on page 147. Cut it into matchsticks 1–2 mm ($\frac{1}{16}$–$\frac{1}{8}$ inch) thick and 4 cm (1$\frac{3}{4}$ inches) long. This is best done by hand, rather than using a food processor or grater, which might reduce the celeriac to a pulp. Sprinkle the celeriac with lemon juice, to keep it white.
◇ Mix the celeriac sticks and the mayonnaise thoroughly in a salad bowl.

INGREDIENTS

450 g (1 lb) celeriac
juice of $\frac{1}{2}$ lemon
FOR THE MAYONNAISE
1 egg yolk
250 ml (8 fl oz/1 cup) grapeseed or peanut oil
5 ml (1 tsp) prepared mustard
40–50 ml (1$\frac{1}{2}$–2 fl oz/3–4 tbsp) white wine vinegar
5 ml (1 tsp) salt
2 ml ($\frac{2}{3}$ tsp) pepper

FIRST COURSE

SERVES 4
Preparation: 5–15 minutes
Difficulty: ★
Cost: ★

UTENSILS

1 bowl
1 balloon whisk
1 salad bowl

◇ JULIENNE OF CELERIAC WITH FRESH TRUFFLES ◇

This recipe is based on an idea of Bernard Loiseau.

◇ Peel the celeriac as described on page 147. Cut it into matchsticks 1–2 mm ($\frac{1}{16}$–$\frac{1}{8}$ inch) thick and about 3 cm (1$\frac{1}{2}$ inches) long. This is best done by hand, rather than using a food processor or grater, which might reduce the celeriac to a pulp.
◇ Cut the truffles into julienne strips.
◇ In a bowl, season the cream with salt and pepper.
◇ Mix the strips of celeriac and truffle thoroughly in a salad bowl. Add the truffle juice and the cream; toss well to mix.

INGREDIENTS

300 g (10 oz) celeriac
50 g (2 oz) fresh truffles
150 ml (5 fl oz/$\frac{2}{3}$ cup) double (heavy) cream
salt and pepper
30 ml (2 tbsp) truffle juice

FIRST COURSE

SERVES 4
Preparation: under 5 minutes
Difficulty: ★
Cost: ★★★

UTENSILS

1 bowl
1 salad bowl

◇ CELERIAC GALETTES ◇

These galettes, a type of pancake, are excellent served with fried medallions of venison, or roast meats.

◇ Peel the celeriac as described on page 147. Cut it into thin slices, about 2 mm (⅛ inch) thick; use a mandolin cutter if possible.
◇ Heat the milk in a saucepan. When it is just simmering, add the celeriac slices and blanch for 5 minutes. Drain them and dry on kitchen paper. Heat the oven to 180°C (350°F/Gas Mark 4).
◇ Butter 4 individual ovenproof dishes. Arrange the celeriac slices in them, overlapping them slightly so that they look like flower petals. Add 5 ml (1 tsp) water and a few slivers of butter to each. Season with salt and pepper and cover each dish with foil.
◇ Bake in the oven for 20–30 minutes. Remove the foil, raise the oven temperature to 200°C (400°F/Gas Mark 6) and allow the celeriac galettes to brown for a few minutes.

INGREDIENTS

300 g (10 oz) celeriac
250 ml (9 fl oz/1⅛ cups) milk
75 g (3 oz/6 tbsp) butter
salt and pepper

SIDE DISH

SERVES 4
Preparation: under 5 minutes
Cooking: 30–60 minutes
Difficulty: ★
Cost: ★

UTENSILS

1 mandolin cutter or sharp knife
1 saucepan
4 small ovenproof dishes
kitchen foil
OVEN
180°C (350°F/Gas Mark 4), then
200°C (400°F/Gas Mark 6)

◇ CELERIAC MOUSSELINE ◇

◇ Peel the potatoes and celeriac as described on page 147. Rinse and cut into quarters.
◇ Put the potatoes into a saucepan of cold water. Bring to the boil and cook for 10 minutes. Add the celeriac and cook for a further 10 minutes.
◇ Drain the vegetables. Put them through a food mill or mash thoroughly.
◇ Add the cream, butter, salt and pepper to the mashed vegetables. Mix well. Reheat gently if necessary.

INGREDIENTS

200 g (7 oz) potatoes
100 g (4 oz) celeriac
150 ml (5 fl oz/⅔ cup) double (heavy) cream
75 g (3 oz/6 tbsp) butter
salt and pepper

SIDE DISH

SERVES 4
Preparation: 5–15 minutes
Cooking: 15–30 minutes
Difficulty: ★
Cost: ★

UTENSILS

1 large saucepan
1 food mill or potato masher

◇ CELERIAC PUREE ◇

This purée is excellent with game, or with turkey and chestnut stuffing.

◇ Peel the celeriac as described on page 147. Rinse and cut into quarters. Simmer for 25 minutes in water with a dash of lemon juice. Drain and reduce to a purée in a food mill or food processor, then sieve to make a smooth purée. Bring the cream to the boil in a small saucepan. Allow to reduce by one-quarter.

◇ In another saucepan, melt the butter and heat until nut-brown. Add the celeriac purée and mix for a few seconds over a high heat. Remove from the heat and add the cream. Season to taste with salt and pepper and mix well.

INGREDIENTS

550 g (1¼ lb) celeriac
a little lemon juice
150 ml (5 fl oz/⅔ cup) double (heavy) cream
75 g (3 oz/6 tbsp) butter
salt and pepper

SIDE DISH

SERVES 4
Preparation: under 5 minutes
Cooking: 15–30 minutes
Difficulty: ★
Cost: ★

UTENSILS

1 large saucepan
1 small saucepan
1 food mill or food processor

•S A L S I F Y•

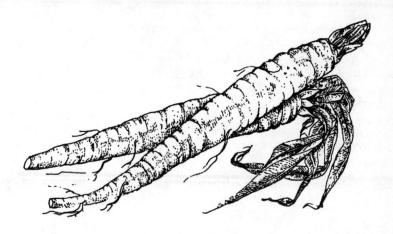

SALSIFY, A ROOT vegetable that is shaped like a long, slender carrot, was much prized in France in the Middle Ages, but it fell out of favour at the time of Louis XIV, who detested it. It was a rather later arrival in England, and is not widely known here.

Smaller salsify roots have the best flavour. Salsify contributes potassium, calcium, magnesium and iron.

◇ BUYING SALSIFY ◇

Salsify may have black or white skin; the flavour of the black-skinned variety is more pronounced. Both types have white flesh. The roots must be firm, smooth and unwrinkled, with no sign of flabbiness, and should be heavy in relation to their size.

◇ PREPARING SALSIFY ◇

Trim away the leaves and root tip, as for carrots, wearing rubber gloves if possible, to avoid staining your hands.

Peel or scrape the roots carefully, removing all traces of skin. You may find this easier if you soak the salsify in cold water overnight. Immediately place the roots in acidulated water, so that they do not discolour.

◇ COOKING AND SERVING SALSIFY ◇

Cut the roots into 5 cm (2 inch) lengths. Rinse and cook for about 15 minutes in blanching liquid – boiling water to which you have previously added the juice of a lemon and 10 ml (2 tsp) flour. This will help keep the salsify white. Drain the salsify before it is completely cooked, and finish it in butter, cream, or roasting pan juices. Serve to accompany meat, with other vegetables such as spinach (see page 154).

◇ To make the chicken stock: chop the chicken carcass into small pieces. Heat the oil in a flameproof casserole or heavy saucepan. Fry the chicken carcass and trimmings, onions, garlic and parsley, until nicely coloured. Pour off the oil, add 600 ml (1 pint/2½ cups) water and deglaze the casserole or pan, scraping the base well with a wooden spatula to loosen any juices and mix well. Leave to simmer gently for about 20 minutes.

◇ Strain the liquid through a fine sieve into a small saucepan and allow to reduce, to make a concentrated and well-flavoured sauce. Season with salt and pepper.

◇ Prepare the salsify and cook in blanching liquid using flour and lemon juice, as described on page 151, for about 10 minutes.

◇ Heat the oven to 200°C (400°F/Gas Mark 6).

◇ Boil the cream until it has reduced by about one-third and is thick and smooth. Season with salt and pepper.

◇ Drain the salsify and place in a gratin dish greased with the butter. Pour over 150 ml (5 fl oz/⅓ cup) reduced chicken stock and the reduced cream and bake for about 15–20 minutes. If the top begins to brown too much, cover with a piece of kitchen foil. Serve hot.

INGREDIENTS

900 g (2 lb) salsify
juice of 1 lemon
10 ml (2 tsp) flour
250 ml (9 fl oz/1¼ cup) double (heavy)
cream
15 g (½oz/1 tbsp) butter
salt and pepper

FOR THE CHICKEN STOCK

1 chicken carcass and trimmings, neck,
wing tips, etc.
10 ml (2 tsp) groundnut (peanut) oil
2 onions, peeled and cut into quarters
2 garlic cloves, peeled and chopped
1 small bunch of parsley, chopped
salt and pepper

FIRST COURSE OR SIDE DISH

SERVES 4
Preparation: 20 minutes
Cooking: 30–35 minutes
Difficulty: ★
Cost: ★

UTENSILS

1 gratin dish
2 small saucepans
kitchen foil
1 flameproof casserole or large heavy
saucepan
1 fine sieve
1 wooden spatula
1 large heavy knife
OVEN
200°C (400°F/Gas Mark 6)

◇ Prepare the salsify and cut it into 8 cm (3 inch) lengths, and cook in blanching liquid as described on page 151 for 10 minutes, using half the lemon juice and the flour.

◇ In a shallow dish, mix a teaspoon of the groundnut oil with the remaining lemon juice, the parsley, salt and pepper.

◇ Drain the salsify and marinate it in the oil and lemon juice mixture for 1 hour.

◇ Meanwhile make the batter: whisk together the egg yolk, beer, flour and salt in a mixing bowl, to make a smooth batter. Leave to rest for 30 minutes.

◇ Heat the remaining oil in a deep-fryer to 190°C (375°F).

◇ Whisk the egg whites very stiffly and fold into the batter. Drain the salsify and coat each piece in batter. Fry in the hot oil until golden brown. Drain well on kitchen paper and salt lightly before serving.

INGREDIENTS

700 g (1½ lb) salsify
juice of 1 lemon
10 ml (2 tsp) flour
1.2 litres (2 pints/1 quart) groundnut (peanut) oil
10 ml (2 tsp) chopped parsley
salt and pepper
FOR THE BATTER
1 egg yolk
10 ml (2 tsp) beer
20 ml (4 tsp) plain (all-purpose) flour
a pinch of salt
2 egg whites

SIDE DISH

SERVES 4
Preparation: 15 minutes
Cooking: 15 minutes
Difficulty: ★
Cost: ★

UTENSILS

1 balloon whisk
2 bowls
1 deep-fryer
1 shallow dish
1 large saucepan
kitchen paper

A simple but delightful dish, in which the sweetness of the salsify contrasts admirably with the slight acidity of the spinach.

◇ Prepare the salsify and cut it into 8 cm (3 inch) lengths. Cook in blanching liquid as described on page 151 for 10 minutes, using half the lemon juice and the flour.

◇ In a shallow dish, mix a teaspoon of the groundnut oil with the remaining lemon juice, the parsley, salt and pepper.

◇ Drain the salsify and marinate it in the oil and lemon juice mixture for 1 hour.

◇ Meanwhile, make the batter: whisk together the egg yolk, beer, flour and salt in a mixing bowl, to make a smooth batter. Leave to rest for 30 minutes.

◇ Wash the spinach and strip away the stalks as described on page 93. Cook the spinach briefly in boiling water. Refresh in cold water and drain well; squeeze it between your hands, or in a tea-towel, to extract as much water as possible.

◇ Heat the oil in a deep-fryer to 190°C (375°F).

◇ Whisk the egg whites very stiffly and fold into the batter. Drain the salsify and coat each piece in batter. Fry in the hot oil until golden-brown. Drain well on kitchen paper, salt lightly and keep hot.

◇ Prepare a *beurre noisette* by melting the butter in a sauté pan, taking care that it does not burn. Keep it over a low heat and skim away the foam that forms, until the butter turns an attractive nut-brown. Cook the spinach gently in the butter, stirring it with the garlic clove impaled on a fork, for extra flavour.

◇ Place the spinach in a heated serving dish and arrange the salsify fritters on top of it. Serve immediately.

INGREDIENTS

550 g (1¼ lb) salsify
juice of 1 lemon
10 ml (2 tsp) flour
1.2 litres (2 pints/1 quart) groundnut (peanut) oil
10 ml (2 tsp) chopped parsley
salt and pepper
450 g (1 lb) spinach
100 g (4 oz/1 stick) butter
1 garlic clove
FOR THE BATTER
1 egg yolk
10 ml beer
20 ml (2 tbsp) plain (all-purpose) flour
a pinch of salt
2 egg whites

SIDE DISH

SERVES 4
Preparation: 15 minutes
Cooking: 15 minutes
Difficulty: ★
Cost: ★

UTENSILS

1 large saucepan
1 sauté pan
1 mixing bowl
1 deep-fryer
1 shallow dish
kitchen paper

PODS AND
·SEEDS·

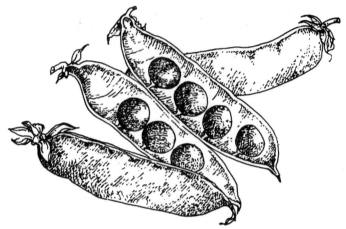

ARCHAEOLOGICAL EVIDENCE HAS been found which proves that the wild ancestor of our garden pea was growing as early as 9750 BC. The Chinese were the first to cultivate peas, followed by the Greeks. Roman invaders brought peas back to western Europe, but to them the pea was rather like the peanut in our society; something that one nibbled as a snack, rather than a major source of nutrition. As the Romans cheered on their favourite gladiator, they ate peas. In medieval England, dried peas were the wages of the poor; in France, until the Renaissance, peas, together with broad beans and cabbages, were the basic diet of the ordinary citizen. Not until the days of Louis XIV did tender green peas become a fashionable dish.

Peas provide protein and carbohydrate with minimal fat, as well as Vitamins A, B and C, and minerals such as potassium, iron and a little calcium and magnesium.

There are two types of peas generally available; those which have to be shelled before eating (and which may be dried for use out of season) and mange-tout (snow) peas, which are not shelled; the entire pod is eaten.

◇ BUYING PEAS ◇

Freshness is all! Look for peas with shiny, bright green pods; avoid any that have whitish spots, as they will probably be hard and floury.

◇ SERVING PEAS ◇

Serve peas especially with poultry, roast lamb, fish, bacon and in certain soups and vegetable mixtures.

◇ PREPARING PEAS ◇

Shell if necessary; you should not need to wash shelled peas. Top and tail mange-touts; you should not need to string them if they are young and tender.

Before buying, plunge your hand into the heap or container of peas; if you feel any warmth, do not buy, as this means that the peas are beginning to ferment. Peas are one of the best vegetables for freezing.

◇ LANGOUSTINES WITH PEAS ◇

◇ Clean the stock vegetables and chop them roughly. Put them into a saucepan with the herbs, add 600 ml (1 pint/2½ cups) water and bring to the boil. Leave to simmer while you prepare the peas and langoustines.

◇ Bring another saucepan of water to the boil and cook the peas for 4–5 minutes. Plunge the peas into cold water, to prevent further cooking, then drain and set aside.

◇ Separate the heads and tails of the langoustines. Shell the tail meat and add the shells to the vegetable stock. Simmer for a few minutes, then strain the stock.

◇ Cut the langoustine tail meats in half lengthways. Heat the olive oil in a large frying pan and fry the tail meats for 2–3 minutes. Remove them and set aside. Pour off the oil and deglaze the pan with 200 ml (7 fl oz/⅞ cup) of the stock. Allow the liquid to reduce slightly, then whisk in the diced butter a little at a time, until the sauce is smooth and thick. Season to taste with salt and pepper.

◇ Add the peas and langoustines to the pan. Check the seasoning again and add the lemon juice. Serve in soup plates, sprinkled with a little finely chopped chervil.

INGREDIENTS

150 g (5 oz) peas (shelled weight)

12 langoustines, total weight about 1.4 kg (3 lb)

90 ml (6 tbsp) olive oil

100 g (4 oz/1 stick) butter, cut into small dice

salt and pepper

juice of ½ lemon

chervil

FOR THE VEGETABLE STOCK

1 onion

1 shallot

1 small leek

1 carrot

1 celery stalk

1 thyme sprig

1 bay leaf

1 parsley sprig

FIRST COURSE

SERVES 4

Preparation: 10 minutes

Cooking: 10 minutes

Difficulty: ★★

Cost: ★★★

UTENSILS

2 saucepans

1 fine sieve

1 large frying pan

◇ GREEN PEA PUREE ◇

◇ Bring a saucepan of water to the boil and cook the peas for about 7 minutes.

◇ Meanwhile, put the cream into a small saucepan and allow to bubble gently until it is smooth and thick.

◇ When the peas are cooked, drain and refresh in cold water, then drain again. Reduce the peas to a purée in a food processor or food mill, then pass through a fine sieve to make a very smooth purée.

◇ Melt the butter in a sauté pan and heat until it is just beginning to brown. Add the purée to the pan still over the heat and mix well. Add the cream, season to taste with salt and pepper and mix again. Turn into a heated serving dish and serve immediately.

INGREDIENTS

400 g (14 oz) peas (shelled weight)
*200 ml (7 fl oz/⅞ cup) double (heavy)
cream*
25 g (1 oz/2 tbsp) butter
salt and pepper

SIDE DISH

SERVES 4
Preparation: 5 minutes
Cooking: 5 minutes
Difficulty: ★
Cost: ★

UTENSILS

1 saucepan
1 sauté pan
1 food processor or food mill

◇ HERRING CROWNS WITH PEAS ◇

Use salt herring (sometimes called Matjes herring), soaked in milk and water to reduce the saltiness, or kipper fillets. Do not use soused herring in this dish.

◇ Cut the herring fillets lengthways into strips about 1 cm (½ inch) wide.

◇ Bring a saucepan of water to the boil and cook the peas for 5 minutes. Plunge them into cold water to prevent further cooking, then drain well again. Season the peas lightly with oil, half the lemon juice, pepper and a little salt.

◇ Peel and finely chop the shallot. Whisk the cream until slightly thickened, then fold in the shallot, the remaining lemon juice, chives and salt and pepper to taste.

◇ Twist each herring strip into a crown shape. Divide them equally among 4 individual serving plates. Fill the centre of each herring crown with peas and coat with the chive-flavoured cream.

INGREDIENTS

8 fillets marinated herring
150 g (5 oz) peas (shelled weight)
10 ml (2 tsp) olive oil
juice of 1 lemon
salt and pepper
½ shallot
*100 ml (4 fl oz/½ cup) double (heavy)
cream*
10 ml (2 tsp) chopped chives

FIRST COURSE OR COCKTAIL SNACK

SERVES 4–8
Preparation: 10 minutes
Cooking: 5 minutes
Difficulty: ★★
Cost: ★

UTENSILS

1 saucepan
1 bowl
1 balloon whisk

◇ Clean the stock vegetables and chop them roughly. Put them into a saucepan with the herbs and 600 ml (1 pint/2½ cups) water. Bring to the boil and cook for about 20 minutes, then strain and cool.

◇ Skin and seed the tomato. Cut the flesh into small dice.

◇ Bring another saucepan of water to the boil and cook the peas for 4–5 minutes. Plunge them into cold water to prevent further cooking, then drain. Set aside a few peas for garnishing and purée the remainder in a food processor or food mill. Pass through a fine sieve to make a very smooth purée, then set aside to cool.

◇ Peel and purée the cucumber in the same way. Mix it with the pea purée in a bowl and add 300 ml (10 fl oz/1¼ cups) of the cooled stock and the cream. Season with salt, pepper and a dash of lemon juice. Cover and chill in the refrigerator.

◇ Ladle the soup into soup plates. Add a little diced tomato and some peas to each plate. Sprinkle with a little chopped basil. Serve accompanied by small croûtons.

INGREDIENTS

1 tomato
150 g (5 oz) peas (shelled weight)
1 cucumber
200 ml (7 fl oz/⅞ cup) double (heavy) cream
salt and pepper
a little lemon juice
a few basil leaves

TO SERVE
small croûtons

FOR THE VEGETABLE STOCK
1 onion
1 shallot
1 small leek
1 carrot
1 celery stalk
1 thyme sprig
1 bay leaf
1 parsley sprig

FIRST COURSE

SERVES 4
Preparation: 25 minutes
Cooking time: 5 minutes
Difficulty: ★
Cost: ★

UTENSILS

1 saucepan
1 food processor or food mill
1 fine sieve

◇ Cook the artichokes, carrots and peas as described for Sauté of Peas, Artichokes and Baby Carrots (p. 161), rubbing the artichokes well with lemon juice to prevent discoloration.

◇ Top and tail the beans. Bring a large saucepan of salted water to the boil and cook the beans until still slightly firm. Plunge them into cold water to prevent further cooking, then drain.

◇ Cut the kidneys into bite-sized pieces. Heat 25 g (1 oz/2 tbsp) of the butter and the oil in a frying pan. Cook the kidneys briskly over a high heat, so that they do not exude liquid and toughen, then drain on kitchen paper. Add the vinegars to the pan and deglaze, stirring well. Allow the liquid to reduce slightly.

◇ Melt the remaining butter in a large frying pan. Add the carrots and cook gently for a minute or two, then add the artichokes, beans and finally the peas. They should reheat, rather than fry. Season with salt and pepper.

◇ Divide the vegetables equally among 4 heated dinner plates. Place some kidney in the centre of each plate and top with a little of the pan juices.

INGREDIENTS

2 artichokes

200 g (7 oz) baby carrots

100 g (4 oz) peas (shelled weight)

juice of ½ lemon

100 g (4 oz) French (green) beans

225 g (8 oz) veal kidneys, trimmed

90 g (3 oz/6 tbsp) butter

10 ml (2 tsp) groundnut (peanut) oil

10 ml (2 tsp) wine vinegar

10 ml (2 tsp) sherry vinegar

salt and pepper

MAIN COURSE

SERVES 4

Preparation: 15 minutes

Cooking: 15 minutes

Difficulty: ★★

Cost: ★★

UTENSILS

1 large saucepan

3 medium saucepans

1 sauté pan

2 frying pans

kitchen paper

◇ CELERY AND GREEN PEA SOUP ◇

◇ Clean the stock vegetables and chop them roughly. Put them into a saucepan with the herbs and 600 ml (1 pint/2½ cups) water. Bring to the boil and simmer for about 20 minutes.

◇ Wash the celery. Cut each stalk into 4–5 cm (1½–2 inch) lengths and cut again lengthways into matchsticks 2 mm (⅛ inch) wide.

◇ Put the celery into a saucepan with 15 g (½ oz/1 tbsp) of the butter and enough water just to cover. Cook the celery until tender.

◇ Meanwhile, bring a saucepan of water to the boil and cook the peas for 4–5 minutes. Plunge them into cold water to prevent further cooking, then drain.

◇ When the celery is tender, remove it from the pan with a slotted spoon. Add 200 ml (7 fl oz/⅞ cup) of the stock to the pan. Mix it with the cooking juices. Dice the remaining butter and add it to the pan, a little at a time, whisking constantly, until thickened and smooth. Return the celery and peas to the pan. Season to taste with salt and pepper.

◇ Serve in heated soup plates, sprinkled with a little chopped chervil.

INGREDIENTS

1 head celery
100 g (4 oz/1 stick) butter
200 g (7 oz) peas (shelled weight)
chervil

FOR THE VEGETABLE
STOCK

1 onion
1 small leek
1 carrot
1 celery stalk
1 thyme sprig
1 bay leaf
1 parsley sprig

FIRST COURSE

SERVES 4
Preparation: 25 minutes
Cooking: 10 minutes
Difficulty: ★
Cost: ★

UTENSILS

3 saucepans

◇ SAUTE OF PEAS, ARTICHOKES AND BABY CARROTS ◇

◇ Break off the stalk level with the base of each artichoke. Remove the tough outer leaves. Cut the top half of the artichokes away, then pare away the leaves until you have almost exposed the choke. Rub the artichokes with lemon juice, and place in a saucepan of boiling water with the remaining lemon juice and salt. Cook for 20 minutes until tender, then remove chokes and quarter artichoke hearts.

◇ Scrape and wash the carrots. Cut them into 2.5–4 cm (1–1½ inch) lengths. Place them in a sauté pan with 15 g (½ oz/1 tbsp) of the butter and enough water just to cover. Cook until the water has evaporated and the carrots are tender.

◇ Cook the peas in boiling salted water for 4–5 minutes, plunge into cold water and set aside.

◇ Melt the remaining butter and cook the artichoke hearts gently. Add peas and carrots and turn to coat.

◇ Turn the vegetables into a heated serving dish, season with salt and pepper and sprinkle with chopped parsley.

INGREDIENTS

2 artichokes
juice of ½ lemon
225 g (8 oz) baby carrots
50 g (2 oz/4 tbsp) butter
150 g (5 oz) peas (shelled weight)
parsley

SIDE DISH

SERVES 4
Preparation: 10 minutes
Cooking: 15 minutes
Difficulty: ★
Cost: ★

UTENSILS

2 saucepans
1 sauté pan

• F R E N C H •
(G R E E N)
B E A N S

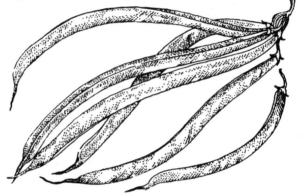

WHAT TREASURES THE conquistadores brought back from the New World! Not least of their discoveries was the kidney bean, brought to Europe in 1510, though it was not until the end of the nineteenth century that we began to eat French (green) beans, green beans with the seeds still undeveloped. The *Herbier de la Famille Robinson*, a nineteenth-century publication, recommended dried, powdered beans as a restorative for the kidneys, and green beans as a remedy for shortness of breath.

They say that Darwin played the trombone to his beans, to hasten their growth, and his enthusiasm is understandable, in view of the bean's many virtues. It is rich in Vitamins A and C, potassium and calcium. Young, tender French beans are good for anyone!

◇ *BUYING FRENCH BEANS* ◇

Freshness is of paramount importance; the very best beans are those that you can be sure were picked the morning of the day you want to serve them.

Buy the thinnest beans possible; they should be smooth and firm and snap crisply when broken.

Allow 150–200 g (5–7 oz) per person as an accompaniment, if no other vegetable is served.

◇ *PREPARING FRENCH BEANS* ◇

Most modern varieties have virtually no strings. Just nip off the tips, then soak the beans in cold water for about 10 minutes, to clean and refresh them.

◇ *COOKING AND SERVING FRENCH BEANS* ◇

French beans are best cooked in 2 stages.

First, bring a large saucepan of water to the boil (allow 4.5 litres (8 pints/4½ quarts) per 450 g (1 lb) beans) and add 2 handfuls of coarse salt. Return to the boil, then add the beans. Cook for 3–10 minutes, according to variety and freshness. The beans should remain firm. Remove the beans and place them in a bowl of iced water. Drain immediately and dry on a tea-towel.

Then just before serving, reheat the beans gently in a little butter.

Serve with roast or fried meat. French beans go well with dishes served in a delicate cream sauce – hearty stews and casseroles tend to overwhelm their subtle flavour. French beans need only light seasoning and are best flavoured with fresh herbs such as tarragon, chervil, parsley or chives.

◇ FRENCH (GREEN) BEAN SALAD WITH CREAM DRESSING ◇

◇ Prepare the beans and cook them in boiling salted water as described on pages 162–3. Drain very well.

◇ Wash the mushrooms, remove the stalks and slice the caps very thinly. Peel and finely chop the shallot.

◇ In a large bowl, mix together the cream, shallot and lemon juice, and season to taste with salt and pepper. Add the beans and mushrooms, mix well and spoon on to individual serving plates.

INGREDIENTS

500 g (1¼ lb) French (green) beans
coarse salt
200 g (7 oz) button mushrooms
1 shallot
100 ml (4 fl oz/½ cup) double (heavy) cream
juice of 1 lemon
salt and pepper

FIRST COURSE

SERVES 4
Preparation: 10 minutes
Cooking: 10 minutes
Difficulty: ★
Cost: ★★

UTENSILS

1 large saucepan
1 colander
1 large bowl

163

◇ SALAD OF FRENCH (GREEN) BEANS AND SMOKED EEL ◇

◇ Prepare the beans and cook them in boiling salted water as described on pages 162–3. Drain very well.

◇ Skin the eel and slice it as thinly as possible. Peel and finely chop the shallot.

◇ Mix together the cream, lemon juice and shallot, and season to taste with salt and pepper.

◇ Divide the beans among individual serving plates. Top them with eel slices and coat with the cream.

INGREDIENTS

550 g (1¼ lb) French (green) beans
coarse salt
200 g (7 oz) smoked eel
1 shallot
200 ml (7 fl oz/⅞ cup) double (heavy)
cream
juice of 1 lemon
salt and pepper

FIRST COURSE

SERVES 4
Preparation: 15 minutes
Cooking: 5–10 minutes
Difficulty: *
Cost: **

UTENSILS

1 large saucepan
1 bowl

◇ FRENCH (GREEN) BEANS WITH SMOKED SAUSAGE ◇

◇ Prepare the beans and cook them in boiling salted water as described on pages 162–3. Drain very well.

◇ Prick the sausage and put it into a saucepan of cold water. Bring to the boil, then simmer very gently for 25 minutes. Drain and cut into slices.

◇ Reheat the beans gently in the butter.

◇ Divide the beans among heated individual serving plates and top with a few slices of hot sausage. Add a dash of vinegar to each serving.

INGREDIENTS

800 g (1¾ lb) French (green) beans
coarse salt
1 smoked sausage
20 g (¾ oz/1½ tbsp) butter
10 ml (2 tsp) red wine vinegar

FIRST COURSE

SERVES 4–6
Preparation: 10 minutes
Cooking: 25 minutes
Difficulty: *
Cost: *

UTENSILS

2 large saucepans
1 sauté pan

164

◇ PUREE OF FRENCH (GREEN) BEANS ◇

◇ Prepare the beans and cook them in boiling salted water as described on pages 162–3. Drain very well.

◇ Reduce the beans to a purée in a food processor, then sieve to make a smooth purée.

◇ Put the cream into a saucepan and heat until reduced by one-quarter.

◇ Melt the butter in a sauté pan and allow it to brown slightly. Add the French bean purée and reheat it, then add the reduced cream. Mix well. Season with salt and pepper and serve immediately.

INGREDIENTS

800 g (1¾ lb) French (green) beans
coarse salt
300 ml (10 fl oz/1¼ cups) double
(heavy) cream
20 g (¾ oz/1½ tbsp) butter
salt and pepper

SIDE DISH

SERVES 4–6
Preparation: 10 minutes
Cooking: 15 minutes
Difficulty: *
Cost: **

UTENSILS

1 large saucepan
1 medium saucepan
1 sauté pan
1 food processor
1 fine sieve

◇ SALAD OF FRENCH (GREEN) BEANS AND CRAYFISH ◇

◇ Prepare the beans and cook in boiling salted water as described on pages 162–3. Drain very well.

◇ In a large saucepan bring to the boil 3 litres (5¼ pints/3 quarts) well-salted water (an egg should be able to float in it). Add the live crayfish, return to the boil and cook for a further 3 minutes. Drain the crayfish and allow them to cool.

◇ Separate the crayfish heads from the tails. Reserve the heads. Shell the tails and remove the thread-like black gut.

◇ Put about half the reserved heads and shells into a mortar and crush them with a pestle, or crush them in a heavy bowl with the end of a rolling pin. Discard the remaining heads and shells. Transfer the crushed shells to a sauté pan. Add the oil and leave over a very gentle heat for 30 minutes so that the oil can take on the flavour of the fish; it should not even simmer.

◇ Strain through a fine sieve and allow the oil to cool. Then use it to make a vinaigrette together with the vinegars, the peeled and finely chopped shallot, and salt and pepper to taste. Heat through gently.

◇ Arrange 3 oakleaf lettuce leaves on each individual serving plate. Top with a layer of beans. Divide the crayfish among the plates. Coat each serving with the warm vinaigrette and garnish with chervil sprigs.

INGREDIENTS

700 g (1½ lb) French (green) beans
coarse salt
50 crayfish or langoustines
250 ml (8 fl oz/1 cup) groundnut
(peanut) oil
10 ml (2 tsp) sherry vinegar
10 ml (2 tsp) wine vinegar
1 shallot
salt and pepper
12 oakleaf lettuce leaves
chervil sprigs

FIRST COURSE

SERVES 8
Preparation: 45 minutes
Cooking: 30 minutes
Difficulty: **
Cost: ****

UTENSILS

1 large saucepan
1 sauté pan
1 pestle and mortar or 1 heavy bowl and
1 rolling pin
1 fine sieve
1 small bowl
OVEN
180°C (350°F/Gas Mark 4)

·SALAD·
VEGETABLES
AND HERBS

Chicory
ENDIVE
168

Radishes
173

Parsley
175

·CHICORY·

ENDIVE

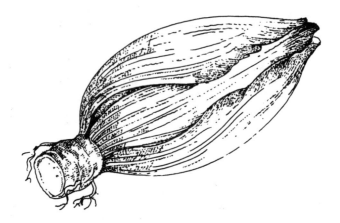

CHICORY (ENDIVE) AS we know it was first grown in 1850, at the Brussels Botanical Garden, where the director discovered the principle of blanching which produces the pale, close-packed shoots we know today.

Belgium and France are the main producers of this vegetable. Belgian chicory is often the better product, by virtue of being more carefully graded and washed.

Chicory needs to be kept in the dark, both during growing and once picked. As the leaves become green, they develop a sharp, bitter taste. The plants are grown in darkness, at a constant temperature. It is a labour-intensive crop, and this fact is reflected in the price. However, as the whole shoot is used, there is no waste.

Chicory is fairly acid, contains potassium and some vitamins and is low in calories.

Chicory can be eaten both cooked and raw. It has a delicate flavour and can therefore form the base of fairly elaborate dishes.

◇ BUYING CHICORY ◇

Choose the whitest shoots that you can find; avoid any that have large quantities of green in their leaves, or browned and rotting edges.

Allow about 250 g (9 oz) per person.

◇ PREPARING CHICORY ◇

As chicory is grown in sandy soil, it needs careful washing. But if the shoots are sound, the sand and soil will not penetrate them and they will not need to be opened out.

To reduce the acid taste of chicory, cut a small cone out of the base, using a vegetable peeler or corer.

◇ COOKING AND SERVING CHICORY ◇

Chicory may be sliced crossways and fried, but braising is the most common way of cooling chicory.

For braising, choose shoots of even size. Wash them and pack them closely in a suitably sized flameproof dish. Add the juice of 1 lemon and a pinch of sugar per 900 g (2 lb) chicory. Add enough water to come two-thirds of the way up the shoots, and bring to the boil.

Cover the surface of the water with greaseproof (parchment) paper and weight down with a plate to keep the chicory in place. Bake for 25–30 minutes in the oven at 180°C (350°F/Gas Mark 4).

When cooked, drain and press well, to extract as much water as possible. The chicory can then be sautéed in butter until lightly coloured.

Chicory is best served as an accompaniment to white meats, game and certain fish.

◇ CHICORY (ENDIVE) MEDALLIONS WITH ORANGE BUTTER ◇

◇ Braise the chicory with the lemon juice and sugar for 25–30 minutes, as described above.

◇ Pare the orange thinly, leaving all the pith behind. Cut the peel into slivers. Squeeze the orange to extract its juice.

◇ Put the peeled and finely chopped shallot, the vinegar, the slivers of orange peel and the orange juice into a small saucepan. Boil until almost all the liquid has evaporated.

◇ Reduce the heat and add the cream. Return to the boil and reduce. Gradually whisk in 4 oz (1 stick) softened butter, a little at a time, to make a creamy sauce. Keep warm in a bain-marie until needed.

◇ Drain and press the braised chicory to extract as much liquid as possible. Cut the shoots crossways into 2 cm (¾ inch) slices. Melt the remaining butter and simmer until it becomes nut-brown. Fry the slices in the *beurre noisette*, taking care that they do not lose their shape.

◇ Arrange the chicory medallions on heated individual serving plates. Coat them with the orange butter sauce and serve immediately.

INGREDIENTS

900 g (2 lb) even-sized chicory
(endive)
juice of 1 lemon
a pinch of sugar
1 orange
1 shallot
100 ml (4 fl oz) malt vinegar
10 ml (2 tsp) double (heavy) cream
150 g (5 oz/1¼ sticks) softened butter

FIRST COURSE

SERVES 4
Preparation: 10 minutes
Cooking: 30 minutes
Difficulty: ★★
Cost: ★★

UTENSILS

1 flameproof dish
1 small saucepan
1 bain-marie
OVEN
180°C (350°F/Gas Mark 4)

◇ STUFFED CHICORY (ENDIVE) ◇

Many different stuffings are suitable for chicory, including leftovers. A little boiled beef, finely chopped, makes an excellent stuffing. Diced scallops sautéed in butter provide a lighter alternative.

◇ To make the vegetable stock, clean and roughly chop the carrot, onion and leek. Put the chopped vegetables, parsley, thyme and celery leaves into a saucepan with 250 ml (9 fl oz/1⅛ cups) cold water. Bring to the boil, then simmer for 20 minutes. Strain.

◇ Wash the chicory. Braise it with the lemon juice and sugar for 25–30 minutes, as described on page 169. Drain the chicory and press it to extract as much water as possible. Cut away the tips and use to accompany another dish.

◇ Heat the oven to 180°C (350°F/Gas Mark 4).

◇ Open out the chicory shoots like flowers and place them in a greased ovenproof serving dish. Arrange a little of the chosen stuffing in each chicory 'flower'. Add a spoonful of vegetable stock and a nut of butter to each one. Put into the oven for a few minutes before serving.

INGREDIENTS

1.4 kg (3 lb) even-sized chicory (endive)
juice of 1 lemon
a good pinch of sugar
50 g (2 oz/4 tbsp) butter
salt and pepper
stuffing of your choice

FOR THE VEGETABLE STOCK

1 carrot
1 onion
½ leek
parsley sprig
thyme sprig
celery leaves

FIRST COURSE

SERVES 4
Preparation: 15 minutes
Cooking: 35 minutes
Difficulty: ★★
Cost: ★★

UTENSILS

1 flameproof dish
greaseproof paper
1 sieve
1 ovenproof serving dish
OVEN
180°C (350°F/Gas Mark 4)

◇ CARPACCIO OF DUCK WITH CHICORY (ENDIVE)

◇ Wash the chicory and cut it crossways into slices 1 cm (½ inch) thick. Melt the butter in a sauté pan and cook the chicory gently for a few minutes, just to soften the leaves slightly. Season with salt and pepper. Drain the chicory well and keep warm.

◇ Slice the duck breast fillets as thinly as possible (this may be easier if the fillets are chilled). The slices of duck should be wafer-thin.

◇ Arrange 5 or 6 duck slices in a fan shape on each individual serving plate, with a little warm chicory to accompany it.

◇ Prepare the vinaigrette and season to taste with salt and pepper. Using a small brush, coat the duck slices with the vinaigrette and serve immediately.

INGREDIENTS

350 g (12 oz) small heads of chicory (endive)
20 g (¾ oz/1½ tbsp) butter
2 duck breast fillets
FOR THE VINAIGRETTE
10 ml (2 tsp) sherry vinegar
10 ml (2 tsp) lemon juice
30 ml (2 tbsp) olive oil
salt and pepper

FIRST COURSE

SERVES 4
Preparation: 15 minutes
Cooking: 5 minutes
Difficulty: ★
Cost: ★★

UTENSILS

1 sauté pan
1 very sharp knife

◇ SCALLOPS WITH CHICORY (ENDIVE) ◇

◇ Peel and very finely chop the shallot. Set aside.

◇ Wash the chicory. Cut it crossways into slices 1 cm (½ inch) thick and loosen the slices so that the chicory falls into individual strips. Cut only the tops of the leaves; do not include any of the centre stem.

◇ Heat half the butter in a frying pan until foaming and add the chicory strips. Cook until transparent, then drain and arrange on heated individual serving plates. Keep hot.

◇ In another frying pan, melt the remaining butter and allow it to brown slightly. Fry the scallops for 15–20 seconds on each side. Season with salt and pepper.

◇ Arrange the scallops on top of the chicory. Return the pan to the heat with the shallot and the lemon juice. Season with salt and pepper and stir, scraping the base and sides of the pan well. Allow to simmer for 30 seconds, then spoon the sauce over the scallops and serve.

INGREDIENTS

1 small shallot
450 g (1 lb) chicory (endive)
90 g (3 oz/6 tbsp) butter
450 g (1 lb) scallops
juice of 1 lemon
salt and pepper

FIRST COURSE

SERVES 4
Preparation: 5 minutes
Cooking: 10 minutes
Difficulty: ★★
Cost: ★★★

UTENSILS

2 frying pans

◇ CHICORY (ENDIVE) FLOWERS WITH CHANTERELLES ◇

◇ Braise the chicory with most of the lemon juice and the sugar for 25–30 minutes, as described on page 169.

◇ Put the chanterelles into a saucepan over a low heat for 2–3 minutes, so that they exude some of their liquid.

◇ Remove the chanterelles with a slotted spoon. Boil the liquid to reduce by half and then add the cream. Allow to reduce further until smooth and thick. Add salt and pepper to taste and a few drops of lemon juice.

◇ When the chicory is cooked, drain it well and press it to extract as much water as possible. Cut away the top third of the stalks; use to accompany another dish.

◇ Open out the chicory shoots like flowers and place on heated individual serving plates. Garnish each chicory flower with chanterelles and pour a ribbon of the chanterelle-flavoured cream around the chicory.

INGREDIENTS

1.4 kg (3 lb) even-sized chicory (endive)

juice of 2 lemons

a good pinch of sugar

200 g (7 oz) chanterelles

200 ml (7 fl oz/⅞ cup) double (heavy) cream

salt and pepper

FIRST COURSE

SERVES 4

Preparation: 10 minutes

Cooking: 30 minutes

Difficulty: ★

Cost: ★★★

UTENSILS

1 flameproof dish

1 saucepan

greaseproof paper

OVEN

180°C (350°F/Gas Mark 4)

·RADISHES·

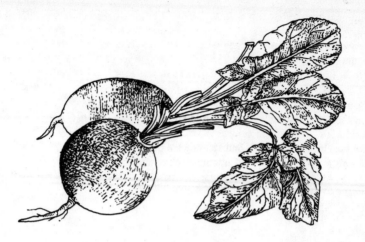

THE RADISH, A cousin of the turnip and the horseradish, is probably a native of China. The Greeks advised taking radishes as a remedy against coughs, to prevent gall-stones forming and to arrest haemmorhages.

Radish contributes potassium, calcium and iron together with Vitamin C and folic acid. We are accustomed to eating radishes raw, as part of salads and hors d'oeuvres, but they can also be delicious cooked.

◇ BUYING RADISHES ◇

Look for medium-sized radishes with a bright, fresh colour. A glance at the foliage will be a reliable guide to freshness, since radish leaves begin to wilt after 48 hours. If the foliage has been trimmed away, it is often a sign that the radishes are past their prime.

Round rather than elongated radishes are best for use in cooking, as they slice better.

◇ PREPARING RADISHES ◇

Trim away foliage and rootlets, then rinse.

◇ GRATIN OF RADISHES ◇

Serve with roast veal or sweetbreads.

◇ Prepare the radishes as described on page 173. Cut into slices 2 mm ($\frac{1}{8}$ inch) thick.
◇ Melt the butter in a flameproof gratin dish and sweat the radishes gently.
◇ Meanwhile, bring the cream to the boil and allow it to reduce by one quarter. Heat the oven to 200°C (400°F/Gas Mark 6).
◇ Turn the radishes into the cream and mix well so that all the slices are coated. Season with salt and pepper and mix again. Return the mixture to the gratin dish.
◇ Bake for 15 minutes. Serve hot.

INGREDIENTS

3 bunches of radishes
10 g ($\frac{1}{4}$ oz/2 tsp) butter
300 ml (10 fl oz/1$\frac{1}{4}$ cups) double (heavy) cream
salt and pepper

SIDE DISH

SERVES 4
Preparation: under 5 minutes
Cooking: 15–30 minutes
Difficulty: ★
Cost: ★

UTENSILS

1 flameproof gratin dish
1 small saucepan
OVEN
200°C (400°F/Gas Mark 6)

◇ GLAZED RADISHES ◇

Radishes cooked this way taste rather like young turnips and can be served with rabbit, duck and other meats that marry well with turnips.

◇ Prepare the radishes as described on page 173.
◇ Put the radishes into a sauté pan, with the butter, sugar and enough water to barely cover. Add a pinch of salt and a grinding of pepper.
◇ Cook over a gentle heat until the water has evaporated, turning the radishes gently from time to time. As they cook, they will lose their bright red colour and become wine-coloured. Serve hot.

INGREDIENTS

2 bunches of radishes
10 g ($\frac{1}{4}$ oz/2 tsp) butter
a pinch of sugar
salt and pepper

SIDE DISH

SERVES 4
Preparation: under 5 minutes
Cooking: 10 minutes
Difficulty: ★
Cost: ★

UTENSILS

1 sauté pan

•P A R S L E Y•

PARSLEY WAS LONG considered the 'Devil's plant' and our medieval ancestors believed it was endowed with malevolent powers. What an injustice towards a plant in fact blessed with so many virtues! Parsley is a tonic and prevents rickets, anaemia and scurvy and is rich in Vitamin A. It also contains plenty of Vitamin C, potassium, magnesium, calcium, phosphorus and iron which is necessary for healthy red blood cells.

It was said that a wad of cottonwool soaked in parsley juice would halt nosebleeds; a mixture of oil and parsley would calm toothache, and a compress soaked in an infusion of parsley would soothe inflamed eyes. In England, it was even believed that parsley kept fleas away!

◇ There are two kinds of parsley; flat-leaved and curly. The flat-leaved variety, known as continental parsley, is considered to have a better flavour.

◇ PREPARING AND COOKING PARSLEY ◇

To make a purée of parsley which will serve as the basis of a variety of recipes: remove the stalks from the parsley and reserve for use in stocks, etc. Bring a large saucepan of lightly salted water to the boil. Drop in the parsley leaves, return to the boil and cook for 4 minutes. Remove the parsley from the pan, drain it and plunge it into cold water to prevent further cooking and preserve its colour.

Drain the parsley again. Reduce to a purée in a blender or food processor, then put through a fine sieve.

This purée will serve as the basis for a variety of recipes.

The sauce may be prepared up to 30 minutes in advance, but the parsley purée should be added just before serving.

◇ Use the parsley to make a purée as described on page 175.

◇ Peel and finely chop the shallots and put them into a small saucepan together with the vinegar, wine and a pinch of salt. Place over a high heat and boil until the liquid has almost completely evaporated.

◇ Add the cream and allow to reduce once more. Reduce the heat and whisk in the butter a little at a time, to make a creamy sauce. Stir in the parsley purée.

◇ Meanwhile, fry the tuna for 5–7 minutes each side, in a mixture of oil and butter. Serve the sauce in a sauceboat, to accompany the tuna.

INGREDIENTS

1 large bunch of parsley
2 small shallots
50 ml (2 fl oz/¼ cup) sherry vinegar
50 ml (2 fl oz/¼ cup) dry white wine
salt
10 ml (2 tsp) double (heavy) cream
100 g (4 oz/1 stick) butter, softened
1 tuna steak, about 700 g (1½ lb)
a little oil and extra butter for frying

MAIN COURSE

SERVES 4
Preparation: 5–15 minutes
Cooking: about 15 minutes
Difficulty: ★★
Cost: ★★

UTENSILS

1 large saucepan
1 colander
1 blender or food processor
1 sieve
1 small saucepan
1 balloon whisk
1 frying pan

◇ CHICKEN WITH PARSLEY ◇

The chicken is stuffed with a mixture strongly flavoured with parsley, then roasted. When the chicken is cooked, you can remove the stuffing, if you like, and spread it on slices of toasted bread, to serve with an aperitif. The parsley will also have flavoured the chicken and its juices.

◇ Heat the oven to 190°C (375°F/Gas Mark 5).
◇ Peel and thinly slice the onions. Cut the tomatoes into quarters. Chop the parsley and mix it with the onions, tomatoes, garlic and salt and pepper.
◇ Stuff the chicken with this mixture; stitch up the apertures so that the stuffing does not escape. Smear the chicken with the butter, then roast in the oven for about 1 hour 20 minutes, until cooked through.
◇ When the chicken is cooked, spoon out the stuffing and use it as described above, if liked; keep chicken warm in low oven. If the stuffing is not sufficiently cooked by the time the chicken is ready, spoon it into a small saucepan. Add $\frac{1}{2}$ a spoonful of chicken juices from the pan and cook gently until the mixture reaches the required consistency.
◇ Serve the skimmed pan juices in a sauceboat, to accompany the chicken.

INGREDIENTS

3 onions
3 tomatoes
2 bunches of parsley
3 garlic cloves, unpeeled
salt and pepper
1 chicken, about 1.4 kg (3 lb)
45 g (1½oz/3 tbsp) butter

MAIN COURSE

SERVES 6
Preparation: 15 minutes
Cooking: 1½ hours
Difficulty: ★
Cost: ★

UTENSILS

1 trussing needle
1 roasting pan
1 small saucepan
OVEN
190°C (375°F/Gas Mark 5)

◇ PARSLEY SOUP ◇

◇ Peel and slice the onion. Wash the leek and cut it into small pieces.
◇ Peel the garlic cloves. Skin and seed the tomatoes.
◇ Heat the oil in a saucepan. Add the onion and leek and cook gently until transparent. Add the tomatoes, garlic, salt and pepper and 1 litre (1¾ pints/1 quart) water. Bring to the boil, then simmer gently for 15–30 minutes, until all the vegetables are tender. Reduce them to a purée in a blender or food processor.
◇ Meanwhile, use the parsley to make a purée, as described on page 175.
◇ Reheat the vegetable soup gently and add 45 ml (3 tbsp) of the parsley purée just before serving.

INGREDIENTS

1 onion
1 leek
4 garlic cloves
3 tomatoes
10 ml (2 tsp) olive oil
salt and pepper
1 large bunch of parsley

FIRST COURSE

SERVES 4
Preparation: 5 minutes
Cooking: 15–30 minutes
Difficulty: ★
Cost: ★

UTENSILS

2 saucepans
1 blender or food processor
1 fine sieve

◇ PARSLEY QUENELLES ◇

◇ Use the parsley to make a purée as described on page 175, chopping by hand, not in a blender or food processor. Sprinkle the gelatine on to 30 ml (2 tbsp) hot water. Immediately whip the cream until it forms soft peaks and fold it into the liquid gelatine. Season with salt and pepper. Add the parsley purée and mix well. Chill in the refrigerator for 1–2 hours, until the mixture thickens.

◇ Wash the mushrooms and slice them thinly. Place them in a large bowl and add the lemon juice to prevent the mushrooms from discolouring.

◇ Put some mushroom strips on each individual serving plate. Dip a dessertspoon in hot water and use it to shape 12 quenelles of the parsley mousse mixture; dip the spoon in hot water again after you have shaped each one.

◇ Arrange 3 quenelles on each plate and garnish each plate with 3 cherry tomatoes.

INGREDIENTS

1 large bunch of parsley, 150 g (5 oz)
5 ml (1 tsp) powdered gelatine
100 ml (4 fl oz/½ cup) whipping cream
200 g (7 oz) button mushrooms
juice of 1 lemon
12 cherry tomatoes, skinned

FIRST COURSE

SERVES 4
Preparation: 10 minutes
Chilling: 1–2 hours
Difficulty: ★
Cost: ★

UTENSILS

1 blender or food processor
1 fine sieve

◇ SCALLOPS WITH PARSLEY BUTTER ◇

◇ Use the parsley to make a purée as described on page 175.

◇ Peel and finely chop the shallots and put them into a small saucepan with the vinegar, wine and a pinch of salt. Place over a high heat and boil until the liquid has almost completely evaporated.

◇ Add the cream and allow to reduce once more. Reduce the heat and whisk in the butter in a little at a time, to make a creamy sauce. Stir in the parsley purée.

◇ Separate the coral from the white part of the scallops. If they are thick, cut them in half horizontally.

◇ Melt a little butter in a non-stick frying pan. Over a very gentle heat, cook the corals for about 15 seconds. Add the white scallops and cook for about 10 seconds on each side.

◇ Put a pool of parsley butter sauce on each heated dinner plate. Divide the scallops and corals among the plates.

INGREDIENTS

1 large bunch of parsley
2 small shallots
50 ml (2 fl oz/¼ cup) sherry vinegar
50 ml (2 fl oz/¼ cup) dry white wine
10 ml (2 tsp) double (heavy) cream
100 g (4 oz/1 stick) butter, softened
450 g (1 lb) scallops, with the coral
a little butter for frying

MAIN COURSE

SERVES 4
Preparation: 5–15 minutes
Cooking: under 15 minutes
Difficulty: ★★
Cost: ★★

UTENSILS

1 large saucepan
1 blender or food processor
1 fine sieve

RICE AND ·LENTILS·

Rice
180

Lentils
186

◆R I C E◆

ALTHOUGH RICE IS the most ancient food crop cultivated by man, having been grown in its present form since at least 4000 years BC, it is a comparatively recent arrival in Europe. It was in 1506 that Vasco da Gama brought rice to the king of Portugal.

Today, rice is grown in the United States (the major exporting country), in Indonesia, China and Thailand. For some centuries now, rice has also been grown in Africa, but the African rice is a less fertile species and consequently not exported. Closer to home, there are rice-growing areas in France, Spain and Italy. After harvesting, rice must be husked before use. Depending on how this is done, different types of rice are obtained: brown rice has only the outer husk removed, and retains a higher proportion of nutrients and vitamins by not being completely stripped. White rice has had the whole of its protective husk removed, and therefore contains fewer nutrients and less fibre.

However it has been treated, rice is an easily digestible food which contains proteins, carbohydrates and vitamins from the B group. It is suitable for all diets and can be served as the basis of many dishes, or as an accompaniment to almost any meat or fish dish. Everyone should eat rice at least once a week: 40–50 g (1½–2 oz) raw weight, or 75–100 g (3–4 oz) cooked weight makes an average serving.

The water in which rice has been cooked is often used to treat diarrhoea, particularly among children.

◇ VARIETIES OF RICE ◇

Long-grain rice is frequently sold pre-treated, which makes it quicker and easier to cook, since it does not stick. Long-grain rice is available from many different sources, but Basmati rice, from Pakistan, is generally considered the best of this type.

Round-grain rice is generally used for desserts.

Wild rice is not in fact a grain at all, but a species of water grass. It is cooked in the same way as rice, and is particularly good in stuffing.

180

◇ *PREPARING RICE* ◇

Always wash rice before use; it is sufficient to rinse it in a sieve under the cold tap. Untreated rice (Asian or European varieties) will need longer rinsing than pre-treated rice.

◇ *COOKING RICE* ◇

Rice may be cooked in a number of ways: boiled; steamed; fried and then simmered (pilaff).

Boiled rice

Bring a saucepan of salted water to the boil. Sprinkle in the rice and stir until the water returns to the boil, so that the rice does not stick. Cook for 16–18 minutes, according to how well done you like your rice. Drain and rinse in hot water.

Steamed rice

This method of cooking rice has two distinct advantages:
◇ not having been in contact with the water, the rice retains all its nutritional value, and cannot break up;
◇ the cooking water can be flavoured with herbs or aromatics, and the cooked rice will be subtly flavoured as a result. For example, to accompany a chicken dish, use verbena to flavour the rice; a lemon-flavoured herb, if serving fish; or thyme to accompany lamb or duck.

Pilaff rice

Peel and thinly slice an onion or a shallot. Fry it gently in oil, butter, duck fat or lard until transparent but not browned. Add the rice and stir until the rice is well coated and beginning to whiten. Add water or stock: the volume of liquid required will be between 1½ and 2 times that of the rice, so remember to measure the rice in a measuring jug before you start to cook it. Add a bouquet garni and salt. Cover and leave to cook for 17 minutes.

Whichever method you use, do not stir the rice after the initial period of cooking. Allow 15–20 minutes' cooking from the time the rice begins to simmer. You may judge by taste (when done the rice is only just firm in the middle) or by appearance (when perfectly done, rice is pure white).

Leave the rice undisturbed for 15 minutes, then fluff up with a fork and add a few slivers of butter.

◇ To prepare the croquettes, peel and mince the onion and sweat it very gently in half the butter in a sauté pan, until transparent. Add the rice and twice its volume of water, plus the chicken stock or the stock cube. Season with salt, cover and cook for 20 minutes, until the rice is tender and all the liquid has evaporated.

When the rice is cooked, remove it from the heat and allow to stand for 10 minutes. Add one of the egg yolks and mix well to bind. Spread the rice out on a baking tray and leave to cool completely. Meanwhile, mix the remaining egg yolks in a bowl with all but 5 ml (1 tsp) of the oil and 45 ml (3 tbsp) water. Spread the breadcrumbs out in a soup plate and put the flour in another.

◇ Shape the cold rice into croquettes. Either cut out small shapes, using a pastry-cutter, or form the rice into small balls. Set aside.

◇ Prepare the tomato coulis: skin and seed the tomatoes. Cut the flesh into small dice. Peel and finely slice the shallot and sweat it gently in the remaining oil and butter. Add the diced tomato, salt, pepper and chopped basil. Cook gently for about 20 minutes, until soft and pulpy, then reduce the mixture to a purée in a blender or food processor.

◇ Heat oil in a deep-fryer to 170°C (325°F).

◇ Dip the croquettes into the flour and shake off the excess, then dip in the oil and egg yolk mixture, then roll them in breadcrumbs, to coat thoroughly.

◇ Fry a small batch of the croquettes in the hot oil for a few seconds, until golden-brown. Keep warm in a heated serving dish while you fry the rest of the croquettes in the same way.

◇ Reheat the tomato coulis and serve in a sauceboat with the croquettes.

INGREDIENTS

FOR THE CROQUETTES

1 small onion

25 g (1 oz/2 tbsp) butter

200 g (7 oz/1 cup) long-grain rice

salt

75 ml (3 fl oz/⅓ cup) chicken stock or ⅓ chicken stock cube

3 egg yolks

45 ml (3 tbsp) groundnut (peanut) oil

about 50 g (2 oz) dried breadcrumbs

about 45 ml (3 tbsp) plain (all-purpose) flour

oil for deep-frying

FOR THE COULIS

300 g (10 oz) tomatoes

1 shallot

salt and pepper

2 small basil leaves

FIRST COURSE

Preparation: under 5 minutes

Cooking: 15–30 minutes

Difficulty: ★★

Cost: ★

UTENSILS

1 sauté pan

1 baking tray

1 pastry-cutter (optional)

1 bowl

1 deep-fryer

1 frying pan

1 blender or food processor

◇ Wash and scrape the carrots, cut them into 5 cm (2 inch) lengths. Wash and trim the leeks. Slice one thinly. Wash the onions. Peel and slice one thinly. Stick a clove into another and leave the remainder whole. Rinse the rice.

◇ Melt the butter in a large sauté pan. Add the sliced leek and onion, season with salt and pepper and cook over a very gentle heat until transparent. Remove from the heat and stir in the rice. Mix well.

◇ Rinse the chicken, then stuff with the rice mixture. Sew up the cavity so that the stuffing cannot escape.

◇ Put the chicken into a large saucepan with the stock. Cover and bring to the boil, then simmer for 30 minutes. Add the carrots, leeks, whole onions, bouquet garni and garlic. Cover and simmer very gently for about 2 hours, until the chicken is cooked through.

◇ Meanwhile, make the vinaigrette by mixing together the ingredients in the order listed.

◇ Remove the cooked chicken from the pan and open the cavity. Place on a heated serving platter and surround with the cooked vegetables.

◇ Warm the vinaigrette gently in a small saucepan, then whizz for a few seconds in a blender or food processor, so that it is emulsified. Serve in a sauceboat to accompany the chicken and vegetables.

INGREDIENTS

100 g (4 oz) carrots
200 g (7 oz) small leeks
100 g (4 oz) button onions
1 clove
200 g (7 oz/1 cup) long-grain rice
20 g ($\frac{3}{4}$ oz/1$\frac{1}{2}$ tbsp) butter
salt and pepper
1 chicken, about 1.4 kg (3 lb)
2.8 litres (5 pints/2$\frac{1}{4}$ quarts) vegetable stock
1 bouquet garni
1 garlic clove
FOR THE VINAIGRETTE
20 ml (4 tsp) sherry vinegar
20 ml (4 tsp) red wine vinegar
salt and pepper
5 ml (1 tsp) walnut oil
45 ml (3 tbsp) groundnut (peanut) oil

MAIN COURSE

SERVES 4
Preparation: 15–30 minutes
Cooking: 2$\frac{1}{2}$ hours
Difficulty: **
Cost: *

UTENSILS

1 large saucepan
1 small saucepan
1 large sauté pan
1 blender or food processor
1 trussing needle and thread (or string)

◇ To prepare the Saffron Rice, peel and finely chop the onion. Rinse the rice.

◇ Melt the butter in a large sauté pan with a lid and sweat the onion very gently, until softened but not coloured. Add the rice, bay leaf, thyme and saffron. Mix well and add 400 ml (14 fl oz/1⅓ cups) water. Cover and leave to cook for 17 minutes, until the rice is tender and all the liquid has evaporated.

◇ To prepare the kebabs, cut the monkfish and salmon into cubes. Shell the langoustines or Pacific prawns. Cut the scallops in half if large. Thread the fish, prawns and scallops alternately on to 4 kebab skewers.

◇ Mix the saffron with a little olive oil and dip the kebabs into it. Allow to drain.

◇ Heat the oven to 220°C (425°F/Gas Mark 7). Heat the grill to high. Grill the kebabs just long enough to seal and brown lightly. Place them in the oven for about 3 minutes, to finish cooking.

◇ Spoon a portion of Saffron Rice on to each heated dinner plate. Top with a kebab and scatter with a few chives. Serve immediately.

INGREDIENTS

FOR THE RICE

1 onion
200 g (7 oz/1 cup) long-grain rice
25 g (1 oz/2 tbsp) butter
¼ bay leaf
1 thyme sprig
a pinch of saffron powder

FOR THE KEBABS

150 g (5 oz) monkfish
150 g (5 oz) salmon steak
4 langoustines or Pacific prawns
4 scallops (white part only)
a pinch of saffron powder
salt and pepper
a little olive oil
a few chopped chives

MAIN COURSE

SERVES 4
Preparation: 15–30 minutes
Cooking: 20 minutes
Difficulty: *
Cost: **

UTENSILS

1 large sauté pan
4 kebab skewers
OVEN
220°C (425°F/Gas Mark 7)

◇ Heat the oven to 180°C (350°F/Gas Mark 4).

◇ Wash the mushrooms, trim away the lower part of the stalks and slice the mushrooms thinly. Peel and thinly slice the shallots.

◇ Place the pork in a lightly buttered roasting pan and roast for 30 minutes.

◇ Add the mushrooms and two-thirds of the shallots to the pan. Return to the oven and allow to cook for a few minutes, until the vegetables have exuded their liquid, but are not coloured.

◇ Remove the pork and vegetables from the pan and set aside. Add 150 ml (5 fl oz/⅔ cup) water to the pan and deglaze, scraping the base and sides well with a wooden spatula. Remove three-quarters of the juices from the pan and pass through a fine sieve. Set aside.

◇ Return the pork and vegetables to the pan, together with 15 g (½ oz/1 tbsp) of the butter, and return to the oven. Cook for a further 50 minutes or until cooked through.

◇ Meanwhile, rinse the rice. Melt 15 g (½ oz/1 tbsp) of the butter in a large sauté pan with a lid and cook the remaining shallot over a very gentle heat. Add the rice and turn up the heat. Cook briskly, stirring, for 2–3 minutes, then add the reserved strained cooking juices, cover the pan, lower the heat and cook for about 15 minutes.

◇ When the pork is cooked, remove it from the oven and wrap it in kitchen foil to keep warm. Remove the vegetables from the roasting pan with a slotted spoon and set aside. Leave the juices in the roasting pan and boil down to reduce slightly if necessary. Just before serving, whisk in the remaining butter, cut into small pieces, until the sauce is thickened.

◇ Place a portion of rice on each heated dinner plate (the rice may be moulded in a ramekin, then turned out to serve, if desired).

◇ Carve the pork and add several slices to each plate. Coat with the pan juices and garnish with the reserved mushrooms and shallot.

INGREDIENTS

150 g (5 oz) button mushrooms
150 g (5 oz) shallots
1 boned and rolled roast of pork, about 800 g (1¾ lb)
50 g (2 oz/4 tbsp) butter
200 g (7 oz/1 cup) long-grain rice

MAIN COURSE

Preparation: 30 minutes
Cooking: 1 hour 20 minutes
Difficulty: ★★
Cost: ★

UTENSILS

1 roasting pan
1 large sauté pan with a lid
1 fine sieve
1 balloon whisk
kitchen foil
1 wooden spatula
OVEN
180°C (350°F/Gas Mark 4)

•L E N T I L S•

Lentils were long considered a poor man's dish of little worth, which never made an appearance at a festive meal. The Jews reserved lentils for times of famine and of mourning; the Greeks considered them a dish suitable for soldiers prior to combat, or for philosophers who sought to detach themselves from the material things of life. The Romans treated lentils as a medicinal plant, and this reputation was maintained until the Middle Ages when, still regarded as food fit only for the poor, lentils were prescribed as part of a restricted and curative diet.

Today lentils have lost this aura of poverty and dullness. They often feature in regional cookery and their considerable nutritional value makes them a useful food for children and for those who do manual work. They contain large amounts of valuable protein and carbohydrate, together with potassium, magnesium, zinc, iron, phosphorous and B vitamins. They are ideal for those following a vegetarian diet. Lentils should be eaten together with grain foods (e.g. rice) so that the proteins in each are complemented for full use by the body. Because lentils are dried it is vital to soak lentils for several hours before using them.

There are various types of lentils, each suitable for different purposes. For the recipes in this book, green lentils are most suitable.

◇ BUYING LENTILS ◇

It is important to use recently harvested lentils, but unfortunately only trial and error, or the location of a reliable supplier, will ensure this. Older lentils will lose their shape during cooking without ever becoming really tender.

◇ PREPARING LENTILS ◇

Pick lentils over carefully, to remove any that are misshapen and any small stones or grit. Wash the lentils well as they are often dusty. Soak for about 2 hours, preferably in tepid water. When the skins begin to wrinkle, it is a sign that the lentils are softening. Although lentils swell when soaked, this is not the primary purpose of the exercise; by softening the skin, the cooking process is shortened and made more effective.

◇ COOKING AND SERVING LENTILS ◇

Place the lentils in cold water, allowing 300 ml (10 fl oz/1¼ cups) water per 100 g (4 oz) lentils. Cooking will take 45–60 minutes, depending on the condition of the lentils. The lentils will be tastier if you also add to the cooking water 1 or more onions, each stuck with a clove.

Lentils dishes are excellent with all types of game, especially partridge, and with all kinds of pork dishes.

◇ CHEF'S TIPS ◇

If at all possible, do not cook lentils in very hard water, since the skins remain stubbornly tough. A pinch of bicarbonate of soda will help, if the use of hard water is unavoidable.

◇ WARM SALAD OF LENTILS WITH CONFIT OF DUCK ◇

Confit de canard, duck cooked gently in its own fat together with some lard, and originally preserved in stoneware storage jars, is a speciality of south-western France. It can now be bought canned, in preserving jars or even vacuum-packed, in French supermarkets and specialist foodstores. Or try making your own, using the method given by Jane Grigson in *Charcuterie and French Pork Cookery.*

◇ Pick over and wash the lentils. Soak them in cold water for 45 minutes. Drain and cook in 3 litres (5¼ pints/3 quarts) water, together with the onions and the bouquet garni, until tender. Drain, discard flavourings and leave lentils to cool.
◇ Make a vinaigrette by mixing together the ingredients in the order listed.
◇ When the lentils are tepid, put them into a bowl, pour over the vinaigrette and mix well.
◇ Wipe each piece of confit of duck with kitchen paper, to remove the excess fat. Remove the skin and wipe again, then cut the flesh into thin strips.
◇ Place the lentils in a serving dish, or divide them among individual serving plates. Top the lentils with the confit of duck strips.

INGREDIENTS

200 g (7 oz/1½ cups) lentils
2 onions, each stuck with a clove
2 pieces confit of duck, preferably legs
1 bouquet garni
FOR THE VINAIGRETTE
30 ml (2 tbsp) red wine vinegar
50 ml (2 fl oz/¼ cup) groundnut (peanut) oil
2 shallots, peeled and finely chopped
salt and pepper

FIRST COURSE

SERVES 4
Soaking: 45 minutes
Preparation: 5–10 minutes
Cooking: 45 minutes
Difficulty: ★
Cost: ★

UTENSILS

1 large saucepan
1 colander
1 large bowl
kitchen paper

◇ Pick over and wash the lentils. Soak them in cold water for 45 minutes. Drain and cook for 45 minutes in plenty of water, together with the 2 onions stuck with cloves.

◇ Meanwhile, scrape the carrots and peel the 100 g (4 oz) onions. Cut both into thick rounds.

◇ Melt the butter in a flameproof casserole. Add the pork and sear it on all sides. When it is beginning to brown nicely, add the chopped vegetables and the garlic. Cook for a further 5–10 minutes, stirring frequently with a wooden spatula.

◇ Heat the oven to 180°C (350°F/Gas Mark 4).

◇ Add the wine and deglaze the casserole, scraping the base and sides well to loosen any sediment. Add the tomato purée and the flour. Mix well, and add enough water to cover the pork. Cover the casserole and cook in the oven for 1½ hours, until cooked through.

◇ When the lentils are almost cooked, drain them and transfer them to a sauté pan. Add a small ladleful of the pork cooking liquid and heat through gently.

◇ When the pork is cooked, carve it and arrange the slices on a heated serving platter. Arrange the lentils around them and serve immediately.

INGREDIENTS

250 g (9 oz/2 cups) green lentils
2 onions, each stuck with a clove
100 g (4 oz) carrots
100 g (4 oz) onions
50 g (2 oz/4 tbsp) butter
900 g (2 lb) boned shoulder of pork
2 garlic cloves, unpeeled
50 ml (2 fl oz/¼ cup) dry white wine
10 ml (2 tsp) tomato purée (paste)
5 ml (1 tsp) flour

MAIN COURSE

SERVES 4
Soaking: 45 minutes
Preparation: 5–10 minutes
Cooking: 1½ hours
Difficulty: ★
Cost: ★

UTENSILS

1 flameproof casserole
1 large saucepan
1 sauté pan
1 colander
1 wooden spatula
OVEN
180°C (350°F/Gas Mark 4)

◇ LENTIL CURRY ◇

This dish is good with veal escalopes, lightly fried in butter.

◇ Pick over and wash the lentils. Soak them for 45 minutes, then drain.

◇ Scrape the carrots and peel the onions. Cut both into 5 mm (¼ inch) dice. Melt the butter in a large sauté pan with a lid and cook the onions and carrots gently until they exude their liquid.

◇ Add the lentils to the pan together with twice their volume of water. Cover the pan and cook gently for 45 minutes, until tender. Stir occasionally, to make sure that the contents of the pan do not stick; add a little more water if necessary.

◇ Heat the oven to 220°C (425°F/Gas Mark 7).

◇ Add the cream and curry powder to the cooked lentils. Bring to the boil and allow to reduce. Season to taste with salt and pepper.

◇ Skin and seed the tomato; cut the flesh into small dice. Tip the lentils into an ovenproof serving dish. Sprinkle the tomato on top and place in the oven for 3 minutes to warm the tomato through.

INGREDIENTS

200 g (7 oz/1½ cups) green lentils
100 g (4 oz) carrots
100 g (4 oz) onions
15 g (½ oz/1 tbsp) butter
150 ml (5 fl oz/⅔ cup) double (heavy) cream
5 ml (1 tsp) curry powder
salt and pepper
1 tomato

MAIN COURSE

SERVES 4
Soaking: 45 minutes
Preparation: 10 minutes
Cooking: 50 minutes
Difficulty: ★★
Cost: ★

UTENSILS

1 colander
1 large sauté pan with a lid
OVEN
220°C (425°F/Gas Mark 7)

◇ CHICKEN CONSOMME WITH LENTILS ◇

◇ Remove any meat from the chicken carcass, and cut it into tiny cubes. If the bird was stuffed, make sure that all traces of the stuffing are removed from the body cavity. Leave the cubes to warm gently at the back of the stove.

◇ Chop the carcass and put it into a large saucepan with 1.7 litres (3 pints/2 quarts) water. Clean and chop the carrots and onions and add to the pan. Bring to the boil, then simmer gently for 45 minutes. Strain, return the liquid to the pan and cook for a further 30 minutes.

◇ Meanwhile, pick over and wash the lentils. Put them into a saucepan with plenty of cold water, bring to the boil and cook for 45 minutes (no preliminary soaking is needed in this recipe).

◇ When the lentils are cooked, reduce them to a purée in a blender or food processor. Add the lentil purée to the hot stock. Mix well and pass through a fine sieve.

◇ Reheat the soup if necessary and add the butter; blend briefly in a blender or food processor. Season to taste.

◇ Just before serving, add the chicken cubes.

INGREDIENTS

1 cooked chicken carcass
100 g (4 oz) carrots
100 g (4 oz) onions
75 g (3 oz/⅓ cup) lentils
50 g (2 oz/4 tbsp) butter
salt and pepper

FIRST COURSE

SERVES 4
Preparation: 10 minutes
Cooking: 2 hours
Difficulty: ★
Cost: ★

UTENSILS

1 large saucepan
1 fine sieve
1 blender or food processor

INDEX